Praise for *This Is Why You're Single*:

"Laura and Angela wrote the fuck out of this book. I loved it. It's really funny and makes me very happy that I haven't been single in 21 years. If you want to laugh and find out what's wrong with you, buy this book."

—Joel McHale, star of *Community* and host of E!'s *The Soup*

"I wish I had this book to run home to after every bad date I've ever been on and laugh. It's like hanging out with your most-trusted best friend—and it would have stopped me from sending a lot of embarrassing texts."

—Meghan McCain, author of *America, You Sexy Bitch* and FOX News contributor

"A new take on old dating issues and sound advice on all of the crazy new ones—like the honest, sarcastic big sister you never had. Keep it on hand until you're happily on your honeymoon—then do your single girlfriends a favor and pass it along."

—Kate Hogan, Deputy Features Editor at People.com

"As a *Bachelor* reject, I say spare yourself a national break-down and buy this book! Modern-day dating makes it very easy to F up any relationship before it's even started, but they've figured it out. God bless. Don't go on *The Bachelor*—read this damn book."

—Jenna Burke, ABC's *The Bachelor* contestant, season 16

"Serious laughs and lessons throughout. Aside from B.O., this book articulates why you keep finding yourself alone on national holidays!"

—Jordan Carlos, panelist on MTV's *Girl Code* and reporter on Comedy Central's *The Nightly Show with Larry Wilmore*

"A hilarious and original take on dating with sketch-inspired stories and advice . . . And no, I have never dated either of them."

—Ali Farahnakian, founder of the Peoples Improv Theater and former *Saturday Night Live* writer

"Laura and Angela are not only funny writers, but wonderful human beings. We like them so much that we are personally endorsing their work even though they refused to give us any money."

—*Jake and Amir*'s Jake Hurwitz and Amir Blumenfeld

"Read this book if you want to get over yourself and under someone better."

—Dr. Alex Schiller, author of *Never Sleep Alone*

Praise for *This Is Why You're Single* (the show):

"An entertaining ride through some of the curiosities and headaches of modern dating, with scenes inspired by real-life dating in New York."

—*The Wall Street Journal*

"Find joy in laughing at these two girls and their ridiculous reasons for being single. They have all the same reasons you have probably thought of, but to scary extremes your sane mind would never let you get to."

—StageBuddy

THIS IS WHY YOU'RE SINGLE

Laura Lane & Angela Spera

Avon, Massachusetts

Published by
Adams Media, a division of F+W Media, Inc.
57 Littlefield Street, Avon, MA 02322. U.S.A.
www.adamsmedia.com

ISBN 10: 1-4405-8884-8
ISBN 13: 978-1-4405-8884-6
eISBN 10: 1-4405-8885-6
eISBN 13: 978-1-4405-8885-3

Printed in the United States of America.

10   9   8   7   6   5   4   3   2   1

Library of Congress Cataloging-in-Publication Data

Lane, Laura.
  This is why you're single / Laura Lane and Angela Spera.
     pages cm
  ISBN 978-1-4405-8884-6 (pb) -- ISBN 1-4405-8884-8 (pb) -- ISBN 978-1-4405-8885-3 (ebook)
-- ISBN 1-4405-8885-6 (ebook)
1. Man-woman relationships. 2. Man-woman relationships--Humor. 3. Single women. 4. Single
women--Humor. I. Spera, Angela, author. II. Title.
  HQ801.L2935 2016
  306.7--dc23
                                    2015025900

This publication is designed to provide accurate and authoritative information with regard to the subject matter covered. It is sold with the understanding that the publisher is not engaged in rendering legal, accounting, or other professional advice. If legal advice or other expert assistance is required, the services of a competent professional person should be sought.
     —From a *Declaration of Principles* jointly adopted by a Committee of the American Bar Association and a Committee of Publishers and Associations

Many of the designations used by manufacturers and sellers to distinguish their products are claimed as trademarks. Where those designations appear in this book and F+W Media, Inc. was aware of a trademark claim, the designations have been printed with initial capital letters.

Cover design by Frank Rivera.
Cover image © Armando Zubieta.
Interior illustrations by Lucie Rice.
Interior design by Elisabeth Lariviere.

This book is available at quantity discounts for bulk purchases.
For information, please call 1-800-289-0963.

Dedication

Dedicated to the people we've had relationships, hookups, make-outs, disappointments, and one-night stands with, including the Olympian, chemist, famous actor, Frenchman, fisherman, fireman, film critic, trust funder, student body president, poker champion, skydiver, surfer, stand-up, magazine editor, newspaper editor, model, minor league baseball player, teacher, teacher's assistant, part-time professor, Ivy Leaguer, two paparazzi photographers, Jesus in a high school production of *Godspell*, Gillette commercial actor, runner-up on *Survivor*, production assistant, professional athlete, politician, revolutionary, DJ, doctor, lawyer, veterinarian, bartender and his bi-curious girlfriend, Hollywood screenwriter, accountant, artist, sommelier, talent agent, press secretary, yacht designer, cellist, and state park employee.

CONT

ENTS

Introduction

You can read opinion pieces on the state of monogamy, listicles illustrating the plight of the single girl GIF by GIF, and studies on the evolution of mating trends—it seems everyone has an opinion on just why it is you are single.

In the following chapters, you will find yourself in a few familiar relationship scenarios, and some less familiar: in a covert meeting with a private eye to background-check a new date; in an intervention for your FOMO; in a pitch meeting with advertising executives to rebrand your dating profile; in a love tryst with a beloved holiday icon; looking for love in the Witness Protection Program; in a nature documentary studying mating patterns at a bar; and figuring out what "this" is while being held hostage in a bank heist.

What do these stories have to do with your love life? They are the real reasons you're single.

Just like how your childhood teacher read you the story of "The Tortoise and the Hare" rather than bluntly tell you not to be a cocky little shit and the story about "The Boy Who Cried Wolf" to teach you that if you lie you will get eaten by a rabid animal, we take a page from Aesop's playbook and present to you these modern-day dating fables. Or dables!

Whether you're looking to lock down that second date, third marriage, eighty-seventh text message, or first three-way, the morals you take away from each chapter will make dating a whole lot more doable, a little less weird and, well, actually pretty fun.

THE
SEARCH

11

TIWYS

Too Many People Are Giving You Advice

The Girl and Everyone She Knows

You've gone on two dates with Derek, who you refer to as Dollywood, so nicknamed thanks to his combination of Tennessee roots and affinity for "big boobies." He just texted you to ask if you want to go to his cousin's wedding with him next weekend in Nashville. "Holy shit," you chant over and over as you do a tiny victory dance on your bed. He thinks you are the perfect wedding date: great at meeting people, a fantastic dancer, an easy traveler, and a pretty face to present to his grandma before she dies. Your self-esteem is through the roof.

Then you pause. And you reflect.

A third date is serious business. Meeting the family is even more serious business. And traveling? Is a third date with Dollywood necessarily a good thing? He's been a hot and cold cocktail of sweet gestures (he sent you chicken soup on Seamless when you were sick) and red flags (he didn't tip!).

You ask the first person you come into contact with for advice.

"It's like, do I actually even like him? Could I see myself having his Dollywood babies some day? Do you think I should go?"

The lady at the post office, to whom you've just poured your heart out for the last forty-five minutes, snaps her gum and sighs. "Ma'am, I just asked what kind of stamps you'd like to buy today."

She quickly adds, "However, if I were you? Hell no."

You are conflicted. You decide to poll your trusted team of advisors.

Ring! Ring! Ring! . . .

"What Should I Do?"

WHO YOU ASK / What He/She Says

YOUR MOM / "If you go away with him, whatever you do, do not sleep in the same bed as him or his family will think you're a tramp. Stay in the guest room. And bring some cookies for the mother! You can't just go there with your hands in your pockets; you were raised right. Hostess gift!"

YOUR BEST FRIEND / "OMG, he is completely in love with you. You have to go. You are going to, like, be engaged and pregnant within a year, I swear. So fun. This is the perfect opportunity to bring up your future and where he sees this going. But also play it cool."*

YOUR BEST GUY FRIEND / "Moving a little fast. Dude sounds like a clinger. Tell him to go suck a dick."

YOUR BEST (GAY) GUY FRIEND / "Honey, it's an open bar and a dance floor, what do you even have to think about? Work it! Just don't drink tequila because you know you turn into a sweaty dumpster when you do. Sorry, you know it's true."

YOUR CO-WORKER / "You know Tim in accounting totally used to work for the FBI, right? Have him do a full background check. He did that for Sharon before her bridal shower and she found out her fiancé once got arrested for doing Quaaludes and attaching clothespins to his nipples in a public park. They still got married, though."

YOUR DAD **/** "Do whatever you want as long as I don't have to pay for it."

YOUR HAIRSTYLIST **/** "That's how I met my ex-husband! He's in prison now. You should go. Anyway, I find an extreme haircut decision prior to an important occasion is always a smart idea. The Lob is totally in. It's the long bob. Let's chop, chop, chop! Also, you should give him a blowie on the plane ride there, I've always wanted to try that."

STORE CLERK AT ANTHROPOLOGIE **/** "Everyone is flocking to Nashville! We did our last catalogue shoot at the Grand Ole Opry and a pig barn. Let me grab you this $768 bespoke denim dress for the wedding. It's for the woman that embodies beauty, strength, and true *joie de vivre*. It's total country-whimsy."

YOUR THERAPIST **/** "It sounds like you are dealing with issues of cognitive dissonance when it comes to this trip with Dollywood. This is usually rooted in repressed childhood memories dealing with emotional attachment. How does this make you feel?"

*What your best friend says to your other best friend: "She is out of her fucking mind if she goes all the way to Tennessee for this goober."

What You Do

You send Dollywood a handwritten three-page note explaining your repressed childhood issues and the trepidation to attend his cousin's wedding. He assumes this means you will not be joining him. To his surprise, you show up at the airport, in a dress you can't afford, with your bags packed. Before boarding, you tell him to go suck a dick. You then, to his surprise again, suck his actual dick in the airplane bathroom. The stewardess asks if you would like a drink and you take one look at a bottle of tequila and begin to sweat.

You arrive at his family home carrying sugar-free cookies (thanks to the full background check, you know his mother suffers from diabetes). You've also been informed by Tim in accounting that Dollywood's browser history includes government conspiracy theories and ukulele porn, a thing you now know exists. You play him a ditty you wrote about the grassy knoll before requesting separate sleeping arrangements. His mom casually compliments your Lob on the car ride to the wedding venue. You've taken advantage of the open bar and are now wasted, trying to show off your moves on the dance floor before passing out under Table 14. Before the weekend is over you dump Dollywood, but tell him you want to have his babies. ●

TOO MANY COOKS

People say it's a bad thing to have "too many cooks in the kitchen." If you aren't the domestic type, it's possible your familiarity with what goes on in a kitchen starts and ends with how many minutes to leave your Lean Cuisine in the microwave, so allow us to explain the origin of this phrase. Imagine you're making a really yummy stew. You ask a cook's opinion and they say add more salt. Smart! Then another says add bananas. Untraditional, but okay! Keep asking different chefs and eventually you have an inedible concoction consisting of marmalade, Snickers bars, cardamom, and an old boot. The same mistake can be made when asking others for their opinion about your love life.

Your head can become clouded when dealing with matters of the heart, so seeking out another opinion is not a bad idea, but you need to curate your decision makers and eliminate excess. An immediate family member is an okay choice, because they tend to be the people who have known you the longest. This gives them context when advice-giving, and, depending on their age, wisdom. But what they lack is usually knowing "what it's really like out there" in the dating battlefield. A best friend is a good person to ask, too, especially since she is likely well versed in current dating politics. But what she usually lacks is any more years of wisdom than you have. Getting the opinion of both someone who knows you well and someone who knows what's up will give you the balanced answer you need.

MORAL OF THE STORY

IT DOESN'T TAKE A VILLAGE

Stick to one or two advisors, maybe a third if you absolutely need a tiebreaker. Beyond that, there are too many conflicting theories and you'll end up with a hodgepodge, Frankenstein's Monster–style idea of how to approach things. Once you ask a million people for their opinion, it's hard to get a million voices out of your head. These voices can tend to drown out rationality. Some of these are people you wouldn't even trust to plant-sit for you, so why are you getting their spin on where you should take your love life? The last big decision most of them felt confident making was voting for the blue M&M in 1995.

When it comes down to it, go with your gut. Your gut may be brain dead, but making bad decisions on your own is the only way you'll really learn to not make them again. It's like the old saying: Fool me once, shame on you; fool me twice, I'll probably ask all my friends for advice but then still see you a third time anyway.

And for the record, a third date is kind of early to be his date to a family wedding. You know, if you were looking for another opinion.

You Call Dibs on Human Beings

The Friends and Foot Locker

You're in the midst of a heated retelling of the injustices you've suffered this week at the hands of your petty roommate and her insistence that she pay a smaller portion of the rent because "technically" your room is one-and-a-half square feet bigger than hers (This is why *you're* single, you cheapskate! You digress.). You're using debate-team-level hand gestures, you're citing references, you're using big words like "verisimilitude"— you are on storytelling fire. And then you stop. You realize your friend, who so graciously invited you out on a shopping spree at the mall to vent, is, in fact, not listening to you at all.

"Claire, are you even listening to me?"

"Oh, sorry, homegirl, I'm manwatching," she explains as she swings her bag over her shoulder and brushes you off.

You stop in your tracks.

"Manwatching?"

"Yes," she confirms. "Manwatching. In case I have to call dibs . . . Ooh—dibs."

Your friend points at a six-foot-tall stunner in a crisp suit with a maroon skinny tie walking out of Ralph Lauren. You eye the subject. He's impressive but you also think she may have to check her gaydar.

"You can't call dibs on a human being."

"Sure you can," she objects.

She points to another man, this one walking out of Foot Locker on the second level. He is most certainly straight (no gay man would be caught dead inside of Foot Locker) and most certainly a catch. He lifts his tanned, toned arm to comb his blond hair back while gliding down the escalator.

"Dibs!" she yells.

"That's not fair," you whine. "You can't call dibs on every hot guy."

She can't have Foot Locker (your potential future husband) *and* Ralph Lauren (your potential future *Girls* viewing companion/GBFF). That's just greedy.

"And what if the person you call dibs on isn't even interested in you?" you add.

"It doesn't matter," she insists. "That happens all the time. There is an unspoken code of honor that all women must follow."

Claire saunters over to Foot Locker (the human, not the store) as you chase behind her. But before either one of you can make a move, he speaks.

"Excuse me, I just moved to the area a week ago and I'm going to meet my mates in a bit to grab a Fosters. Do either of you lovely ladies happen to know a good spot to grab a few?"

Mate? Fosters?! Holy shit, he's Australian. And holy shit, he just got a whole lot sexier.

You tell Foot Locker about this super-chill pub down the block. See what you did there? You said "pub" and not "bar" because foreign guys are into that and you're a goddamn cultured goddess. You slip your hair out of its rubber band and run your fingers through it. Your friend asks where he's from. "Malibu," he jokes. You both laugh. Your friend laughs too, but isn't sure why. Oh, your silly, uncultured friend.

A couple of Steve Irwin references later (RIP), and you and Foot Locker's chemistry is so effortless that you would have aced it junior year of high school. Claire is enraged because she's certain you're about to break the Dibs Code of Honor and now you're stuck with an even bigger issue: Foot Locker is obviously into you. Your friend clearly called dibs on him. You've got yourself into one fickle, fucked-up, non-love-triangle triangle over a guy you're not even sure you'll see past the night. But even if you don't ever see him again, you still want to go for it because, after all, he's *Australian*.

Foot Locker. Friend. Foot Locker. Friend. Foot Locker. Friend. Your eyes tick-tock back and forth between the two. Foot Locker pulls out his phone and starts to hand it to you. He wants your number. It's the moment of truth. You're starting to feel like Meryl Streep in *Sophie's Choice* when out of the corner of your eye you spot a tall, broad-shouldered, and bespectacled man walking out of the Apple Store. Like a knee-jerk reflex, you lunge forward.

"Diiiiiiibs!" you scream, your speech slurred from trying to re-create a dramatic slow-mo action sequence.

You pant and grin triumphantly, proud to have mastered this whole Dibs Code of Honor thing. You stroll over to Apple (the human *and* the store), leaving a pleasantly surprised Claire and a befuddled Foot Locker behind. Before you can claim Apple as your dibs conquest, however, he reaches his hand out and clasps the palm of his significant other, who is following closely behind and who is, more importantly, not you.

Dibs. It's harder than it looks. ●

The History of

King Henry VIII & His Six Wives

Henry had a bit of a dibs addiction. He just couldn't stop calling dibs on all the hot lasses. Except one tricky thing about the dibs rule—calling shotty on more than one cute girl at a time can have its downside (particularly for those cute girls at a time when beheadings were easier than divorces). The takeaway? If you know you're some egomaniac's dibs sloppy seconds (or sloppy sixths), hold on to your cranium and run. Run away fast.

Romeo & Juliet

Everyone knows the greatest love story of all time: *Romeo and Juliet*. Can you believe it all started with the balcony scene? "O Romeo, Romeo, wherefore art thou Romeo?" . . . Hold up, honey, we're not talking about *that* balcony scene. Here's the subplot Shakespeare edited out for time: Juliet had a best friend named Bridgette who actually called dibs on Romeo first. Bridge and Rom met at a ball the week before Jules came into the picture (they both liked the same harp trio and engaged in really funny banter about Rom's sword). Not wanting to betray the dibs rule, Ms. Capulet pushed her best friend to her death . . . off a balcony. Really dark stuff, right? Unfortunately for Juliet, karma is a bitch and we all know how *that* love story turned out.

Dibs Gone Wrong

Helen of Troy & Paris

A disrespect of the dibs rule can end in bloodshed. In the case of bomb-shell Helen of Troy, her husband, King Menelaus of Sparta, had most definitely called dibs on her (uh, they were married). Paris, son of King Priam of Troy, got a mad crush on her, abducted her, and brought her to Troy. Subtle move, brah. The Spartan king was so pissed about the dibs diss that he started the Trojan War and destroyed all of Troy. Tough times.

Adam & Eve

There was really no issue here. With no friends and no competition there was no problem. To be honest, this was actually more of a reluctant hookup situation. Ever told a guy you wouldn't go out with him even if he was the last guy on earth? That line can be traced back to when Eve told Adam, "I won't go out with you even though you're the first guy on earth!" But eventually he wore her down, they called dibs on each other, and the rest is history.

GUYS AREN'T DIB-ABLE

Human beings cannot be called dibs upon. Despite endless amounts of evidence to the contrary, it turns out that many men have original thoughts, feelings, and emotions all their own. The wheels are turning in those pretty little noggins, and there is nothing much that you or your friend can do to steer those wheels in a direction different than their due course . . . and other driving metaphors.

THINGS YOU *CAN* CALL DIBS ON:

- Sitting shotgun. *Dibs!*
- The last tortilla chip in the chip bowl. *Dibs!*
- The window seat when booking a flight. *Dibs!*
- That cute puppy at the rescue shelter. *Dibs!*
- A pair of shoes at a sample sale. *Dibs!*
- The single barstool at your friend's mediocre open mic. *Dibs!*
- A piece of gum (actually, you should split it if you're a good friend, so we take this back).
- The last sheet on a lint roller. *Dibs!*
- The right or left side of the bed. *Dibs!*
- The side of the table with a cushioned bench at a restaurant. *Dibs!*
- Mirror space in a public restroom. *Dibs!*
- The *Vogue* magazine at the nail salon. *Dibs!*
- The only stapler at work. *Dibs!*
- The last piece of toilet paper when you're camping. *Dibs!*
- Your grandma's wedding ring when she dies. *Dibs!*
- The side of the Oreo with frosting on it. *Dibs!*

MORAL OF THE STORY

THINK BEFORE YOU DIB

Just remember: One day the shoe could just as easily be on the other foot (sneaker pun!). Sure, Foot Locker was into you, but next week Lacoste, who you totally had your eye on, may be feeling your friend instead.

So sit down with her and talk it out calmly. Explain to her that sometimes in life there are indeed things you can call dibs on, but free-thinking, living beings are not one of them. So smooches, love you, and may the best bitch win.

TIWYS

You Want a Great "How We Met" Story

The Grandparents and the Snapchat

It's the future. You've grown into a dignified silver foxy lady. You pay for everything using your thumbprint. There are roughly seventy-two different video streaming sites—each one offers shows you've been wanting to watch and each one charges a different monthly fee. There's no electoral college. Global warming has rendered the weather out of control. But don't worry, you're not single.

You're at home with your future grandchild, who is just begging to know all about your romantic courtship. "Tell me how you met," she asks, as she adjusts her Wi-Fi hotspot beanie to order a few panuffins (a pancake-muffin hybrid) from the breakfast drone. You think fondly back to when the hybrid food craze was still a novel idea.

"Commencing panuffins," you hear from the robot voice in the sky, as the thump of the panuffin bag lands on your front door.

Your main squeeze, now known as Gramps to the rest of the family, begins to explain your adorable love story.

"Youngin', you don't know anything about romance. Back in our day, things were different! It wasn't so complicated. When you found a young lady you liked, all you had to do was stick your thumb down on her pretty little face and make sure ya swiped right . . . on Tinder."

Grandchild has heard of this antiquated technology. She's pretty sure she remembers learning about this mating custom in her Pre-K anthropology course (kids in the future are crazy smart).

"That's right!" you tell the child, as you turn on some of your favorite oldies music, Beyoncé and Taylor Swift. "Swiping right meant you wanted to message the person. And you didn't swipe right for just anybody. Only someone real special."

What you don't disclose is that by "someone real special" you mean that Gramps had Warby Parker glasses, six-pack abs, and access to his parents' HBO GO account. That was kind of your thing back in the day. Gramps thought you were "someone special" because of your obsession with Neil deGrasse Tyson, your love of dancing, and the strategically angled cleav in your profile pic. That was kind of his thing back in the day.

"We both liked playing Candy Crush, were in the 21–35 year-old age bracket, and were both part of a radical movement," Gramps adds.

Your tablet-smart grandchild guesses things like Occupy Wall Street, WikiLeaks, and the Ferguson protests. But then you explain how you were both on the front lines of that twenty-two-day vegan challenge that was sweeping the nation.

"I nearly skipped right over your grandfather's photo because I wasn't sure which one he was," you remember wistfully. "He had a group photo as his main picture. But then I swiped through and saw his shirtless selfie and I was smitten."

Gramps explains his whole plan. "I knew that a woman with patience would take the time to tap on the photo and see what other photos I posted. It was a test, and her patience paid off!"

You remember how you accidentally swiped left instead of right, rejecting the future love of your life. You were devastated! You tried to change your Tinder proxy settings but to no avail. You thought you might never see him again. You prayed and you prayed the shirtless selfie would turn up in your rotation again.

"I waited seven long, long . . . "

"Months? Years?" asks your grandchild in anticipation.

"Minutes," you sigh. "It felt like forever. But then there he was."

"That's when we finally decided to go on an actual date. Your grandmother had a great personality," Gramps says. "Such wit and charm!"

Your offspring is certain this is when you fell in love. Oh, the romance! What you don't explain is the part about how you really sealed the deal when you Snapchatted a photo of your boobs on the taxi ride home (back when those babies were still at your chin!). Of course, being the classy dame that you were—are—you only let the titty pic show up for four seconds, whereas most sluts would let their photos go the maximum Snapchat ten seconds before disappearing. Damn hussies! You knew he wouldn't buy the cow if you Snapchatted the udders long enough for a screengrab.

"After our first date, I poked her," says Gramps.

"On Facebook? So retro!" says your grandchild.

"No, with his penis. In my vagina," you tell her, more bluntly than you intended. You knew you'd have to have this talk at some point. You try to soften things.

"#relax," you say. "It was no biggie."

Your now-embarrassed grandchild tries to change the subject. "No one uses hashtags anymore! Ugh, you guys are so old."

"Just you wait," you tell her. "#onedayyouwillfallinlovetoo." ●

SO, LIKE, HOW DID YOU MEET?

It's the most common question you'll be getting any time you bring a man along to one of your friend's parties; as soon as you change your Facebook relationship status; or the next time you tell the delivery man, "No sir, the spaghetti Bolognese and bucatini carbonara are not both for me . . . this time."

You might fantasize various "meet-cutes" that run the gamut from the traditional ("We live in the same building!") to the highly unlikely ("We met midair while skydiving!") to the straight-up impossible ("He's Santa Claus's son and I'm Jewish!"). But those aren't your stories. Those stories only happen to couples in the *New York Times* wedding section, on Hallmark Channel Christmas rom-coms, and in serial killer depositions.

You, on the other hand, will most likely meet your future love on a dating website or app (this is also true if you end up a sixty-year-old spinster and the loves of your life are six cats because it's highly likely you found them on an animal shelter website. #adopt), because that's just how you meet people (and cats) nowadays.

As history has shown, How We Met stories get less romantic with each generation. Your great-grandparents wrote love letters back and forth during the war (What war? Any war, people. There was always a war.) and we all know that nothing is more romantic than life and death and a sexy nurse outfit. Your grandparents met when he accidentally delivered a newspaper to the wrong house on his bike route, while your dad made your mom a mix tape when they were just friends in a bowling league.

Now? Telling people you stuck your thumb down on your boyfriend's face and swiped right (adorable?) just doesn't have the same zest you were hoping for. You want a perfect How We Met story. And while social stigmas about online dating are a thing of the past, your subconscious still believes that only people with social anxiety, Craigslist killers, and hipsters need to use the Internet to meet someone.

But think of it this way: If there was a party every eligible bachelor your age within a ten-mile radius was attending and you were invited to go, would you say, "Nah, I'm cool"? No, you would not. You would go. Well, there is such a party happening on your phone and it's (usually) free to get in.

"HOW WE MET" LIES THAT NEVER WORK

- "We met on Hingeeee . . . hiking. Hitchhiking. I met him hitchhiking. Yep, I used to be sort of a drifter. No car, no shoes—just a modern-day hobo, really. I was . . . homeless. One day, I got into a knife fight and won a can of beans, and that's when I decided it was time to see the world. I packed up my belongings in a handkerchief at the end of a stick and who should pick me up at the tollbooth on I-90? Your son."

- "We met on Matchhhh . . . ress shopping. Mattress shopping. His entire body was bitten up by bedbugs and I was bitten by the love bug! It was a match-ress made in heaven. Pun intended."

- "We met on OKCupidddd . . . oralll. O.K. Corral. That's right, we met at the O.K. Corral, the site of the most famous gunfight in the history of the Wild West. I was in Arizona participating in a Wild West re-enactment and who happened to be playing the part of sexy lawman and deadly gunman Wyatt Earp? This guy right here!"

- "We met on Tinderrrr . . . ella's castle. Cinderella's Castle at Disneyland. Sorry, I have a bit of a lisp sometimes. I was trying to find my inner child and he just had a craving for one of those clam chowder bread bowls near the Pirates of the Caribbean ride. It was like a real-life fairytale."

- "We met on Eharmonyyyy . . . ica playing. Harmonica playing. He was my harmonica coach. Yep, I was trying to learn the harmonica. It's a little secret talent that I have. We both have! Hard to believe my quarterback, frat-brother bf is just your modern-day Bob Dylan. But it's true."

- "We met on Christianminglll . . . Christina Milian introduced us. That's right. The singer of the 2001 hit song 'AM to PM' introduced us. Not much more to say."

- "We met on JDaaaaaate . . . shopping. We were shopping for dates. As in the fruit. At the farmers' market. I was making a date pie for a, um, *quinceañera*. Date pies are very popular at *quinceañeras*. And he was buying them to eat. He's all about that fiber! His bowel movements are extraordinarily regular."

MORAL OF THE STORY
DON'T JUDGE A RELATIONSHIP BY ITS STORY

When you tell people your story, it's all about your delivery. If you believe your story is a real-life fairy tale, so will everyone else. Your grandchild will only dream of having a story as nauseatingly perfect as yours. There is no reason for you to look down on these seemingly unromantic modern dating practices because you're holding out for that perfect story so you can call into Delilah's Lite FM radio show and have her dedicate you a love song. No! Use all of the tools, websites, apps, friends, family, co-workers, and boob selfies at your disposal to find your dream guy. Because at the end of the day, it doesn't matter how you met. It's that you met. Oh my god, we're tearing up just thinking about how in love you are going to be soon!

A few of these tears are also because we feel really bad for you . . . the road to true love will be lined with a lot of ugly dick pics.

TIWYS

You Travel in Packs

The Nature Documentarian and the Pride

Reginald Goodwell III is a world-renowned nature documentarian and *National Geographic* coverboy. He has devoted his entire life to the study of pack hunters. Reginald knows that wolves urinate and defecate to mark their territory. He knows that African lions have penile spines that induce ovulation. But what he does not know is how a human male asks a cute human female out for a latte. He vows to find out how on his next expedition.

Camouflaged in a fitted plaid button-up and Toms slip-ons, he enters a pub on the Lower East Side, where you and a group of friends are conversing over a round of vodka seltzers. The perfect specimens. In his hushed British voice, Reginald crouches behind a leather booth and narrates the scene into his digital recorder.

Hour One

The North American single human female—one of the most complex animals on the planet. Agile, sharp-witted, aggressive. In the sweeping wilderness of Lower Manhattan, this majestic creature makes her presence known under the cover of darkness. She is always joined by a large, tight network of like-minded friends who communicate through scent, sound, and text message only.

These highly territorial creatures have gathered in an impenetrable circle. They have strategically plotted this gathering to take place in a location with easy access to alcoholic beverages. Clever girls! I initially imagined this circle formation was for thermodynamic benefits because most animals hunker down together for warmth. I have come to learn that this is actually a unique hunting tactic indigenous to single girl packs—the huddling together allows them to hear each other's stories over the loud music, while simultaneously positioning themselves to see over each other's shoulders. This move also provides both protection from douchey predators and a heightened ability to "call dibs" on nearby hunky prey.

I can observe the pack engaging in friendly greeting customs. Similar to how in the animal kingdom a loved one may be greeted with a sniff of the butt, in the single-girl kingdom friends are met with a compliment on how great their butt looks.

Hour Two

Crikey! It looks like a congenial male is slowly approaching the pack. He is right to be cautious and slow, as he is entirely outnumbered. Bear in mind, these creatures are prone to acts of random aggression, not unlike the spotted hyena of the Serengeti. The nonthreatening solo male is strategizing and seems to be attempting to infiltrate through an opening in the pack's circle so that he may buy his female of choosing a drink, a generous offering of resources. He slowly approaches the most colorful in the flock, who is swaying about in a neon pink crop top.

Zoom! Away he runs. The little bugger was frightened away by a sudden burst of unfamiliar sounds by his target's packmates. The ladies are currently yapping in a frequency distinguishable only to each other. These yaps can also be referred to as "inside jokes" and prove a successful tool in alienating newcomers to the fold. You can tell by the females' erect postures and open mouths that if an outsider should, in fact, approach, they will take offense and attack, assuming this intruder is trying to claim a member of the pride for his own.

LION PACK

Kings of the jungle.

Find new food by following circling vultures.

Hunts big boars.

Separated only when some are placed in a zoo.

Killer nails.

Occasional man hunter.

Primarily nocturnal.

Intimidates opposing packs by the color and size of their mane.

SINGLE GIRL PACK

Queens of the night.

Find new food by following @SeriousEats.

Hates big pores.

Separated only when some get caught up at coat check.

Hour Three

In the distance I can hear howls of "Where is Melissa? Oh god, where is Melissa? She always does this!" The girls are in search of their sloshed friend, Melissa, who I currently spy feebly attempting to get a sip of water from the hydration station.

This poor little darling has been separated from her pride and is unaware danger is lurking in the form of an average-looking, carnivorous, dodgy fellow who is most definitely in heat. The sweaty wanker, in a pastel pink polo, sputters the words: "Want to come back to my place and see my art collection?" In her weakened state, she is no match for this beast of prey.

Blimey! Melissa's protectors swoop in. This pack is stealth and cunning, pacing the attack just right. I've learned in my travels that a separated baby buffalo attacked by lions can be saved when the re-organized herd rallies around to rescue the weakling. In a similar fashion, the single girl herd corners the aggressor and attacks him with fierce questions. "Are you here with friends? Where are they? Why does your hair look like that?" The predator is too exhausted to fight back. A vicious killing.

My evening spent among these huntresses has proved more daunting than the six years I spent living in the damp, desolate swamps of New Guinea with saltwater crocodiles. But it's all just a part of nature. ●

PACK PRINCIPLES

There are three common reasons for traveling in a pack:
1. Women think girls' nights are fun (they are!).
2. Women don't like leaving other women out (this is a good thing!).
3. Women think going out with a big group of other hot women will make them look more attractive by association, as in "I am as hot as my hot friends" (not true!).

RULE OF THREE

No one likes to be outnumbered. Men have a rule of three: More than three women in a group, and it is highly unlikely that a guy will approach. It is frightening enough to open up and face rejection from one girl you've just met, let alone an entire gaggle.

This is one time in which a jury of your peers is a bad thing. A guy just wants to buy a girl a drink and is suddenly faced with the prospect of getting the approval of an entire group. You may think your friends are very nice and nonjudgmental people, but the truth is that you could be hanging out with an entire convent's worth of nuns and a man would still think twice about approaching.

There are, of course, advantages to having an entourage. There is safety in numbers and just like joining the army, it's good to know no (wo) man will be left behind. Your friends have your back and will stop you from doing something stupid, like walking barefoot on a bar floor that will probably give you Coxsackie . . . or going home with someone with a ponytail.

MORAL ***OF THE*** ***STORY*** **BIRDS OF A FEATHER SHOULDN'T ALWAYS FLOCK TOGETHER** The answer is not to cancel girls' night. It's fun to go out with your friends and you should do it whenever possible. But once you're out, try grabbing one friend and taking a walk around the bar apart from the rest of your group. A pair is a manageable, friendly number and it's much easier to find a couple of cute, single, successful start-up CEOs than a half-dozen of them.

TIWYS

You Don't Know How to Meet People IRL

The Girl and the Missing Words

You're standing alone in some grimy dive bar because your friend took the uptown train instead of the downtown train. Now she's halfway to the Bronx and you're halfway through your pilsner. While your friend is on her metro odyssey, you do the one thing you find most comforting: You stare down at your phone.

No cell service. Goddamnit. What are you supposed to do now? There's literally no one to talk to.

Sure, there are at least half a dozen good-looking guys scattered throughout the bar, but they're complete strangers! With no dating profile to scan, how will you open up with your go-to one-liner about the mutual friends you have or that one vital interest you both share: liking *Arrested Development*?

You're about to leave the bar and head home, when a real human male approaches you.

"You look like you could use a refill," he says, eyeing your nearly empty brew.

You look him up and down, noticing his fitted slacks, navy blue sweater, and sideswept chestnut-colored hair. He's normal, totally your type, and you didn't even have to sort through a thousand profiles to find him.

You immediately tense up. Without having seventeen selfie options to send him of your perfect angle (looking to the right, chin two inches down, angled at two o'clock), you fear he isn't getting the best first impression of how beautiful you actually are. You begin to tilt your head to various degrees, hoping that when you land on your perfect angle, it will just feel right. You don't feel it.

"Yes. Please," is all you can muster.

He introduces himself as Cameron and asks if you live around the area. This is where everything goes downhill. With all previous guys, you've had the luxury of screenshotting your conversations and getting the input of your five funniest friends so you can have a hilarious response to mundane questions like this. But here you are in person and your brain has gone into loading mode.

You stand catatonic. You are completely immobile. Before you can answer, twenty-five minutes have gone by and drool is starting to run down your chin. Cameron is Googling "stroke symptoms" and yelling for help.

You see people moving and talking, but the sounds are muffled and the actions are blurred. At this point thirty minutes have gone by. You're still brainstorming the best response to Cameron's question: "Do you live around the area?"

"I've got it!" you think to yourself. "Maybe I can answer him and say something witty like, 'Of course I live nearby. I make it a point to never make my living quarters more than fifty feet away from an establishment with a solid selection of overpriced brews and a vintage dartboard.' . . . That will give off the vibe that I am self-aware enough to reference the ridiculous price-points but cool enough to be down for a little competition. Hmmm . . . I wish I could just run this by Nicole first. She would totally know what to say. Maybe I should mention the pool table instead? Hmmm . . . Tough call."

You decide to go with your original idea of mentioning the dartboard (first idea, best idea), but just as you open your mouth an ambulance pulls up. You get strapped to a gurney, and a neck brace is placed on you while a man shines a flashlight into your eyeballs.

"Can you hear me?" the EMT shouts.

"Pool table," you respond in a drawn-out monotone voice. "I mean. Dartboard."

"It's definitely a stroke," the EMT announces. "She's confused. Not making sense. Does anyone here know her?"

The patrons shake their heads no.

"So sad," Cameron says as he moves on to a brunette at the bar. ●

GOING IT ALONE

Nine out of ten misdiagnosed stroke victims are really just a result of a girl meeting a guy in real life and taking too long to think of a witty response. You don't have your writers' room of girlfriends to help you along in person. No siree, you are a Lone Ranger. You must go this trek Han Solo. Just like how God would only give Moses the Ten Commandments after he hiked up Mount Sinai alone (it was no Laurel Canyon), this is one of those things you have to do on your own.

When you're finally fed up with getting sincere offers from foot fetishists on Match.com and swapping pics of your genitals with guys on Hinge, never fear! Follow this step-by-step guide for what to do when you are ready to meet potential dating prospects in person.

STEP 1: GROOMING

One of the most beautiful treasures that technology has gifted us is the Instagram filter. A little X Pro-II plus the right angle could make Danny DeVito look like Rihanna. The truth, however, is that you cannot hide behind a beautiful profile picture in the real world. So be sure to throw on a little lipstick and reapply that deodorant if you're heading out for a night on the town. Here's the thing: Some guys go for the whole no-makeup, unshaved-armpits yoga chick and others are looking for a pageant-ready diva with fake eyelashes. Do what makes you feel good, confident, and not smelling like a Starbucks bathroom stall. (Here's one tip every sister can use: If your face gets oily, those wax seat covers in bathroom stalls are great oil blotters. Trust.) Keep in mind that the real world provides its own sort of filter in a way: dim bar lighting. The idea to keep bars dark was no doubt proposed by a mustachioed lady too lazy to get threaded.

STEP 2: MEETING

If you want a chance at meeting anyone, leave your phone in your purse and attempt eye contact with interesting-looking strangers (play a staring game, you'll definitely win!). Great places to position yourself for maximum interaction include:

- Next to a lone guy ordering drinks at the bar (opener: "Should bartenders really get a fancy title like 'mixologists' just for putting lavender in every glass?").

- Outside talking to the only other nonsmoker (opener: "E-cigarettes are the new fedora.").

- The bathroom line, where, yes, you actually might meet more loud drunk girls than cute dudes. But it's hard to make new friends in your grown-up years without joining an intramural softball league, so your communication skills shouldn't show a gender bias (closer: "Call me, girl!").

CONVERSATION STARTERS

- Would you rather go bald or go blind?
- Hey, remember S Club 7?!
- When was the last time you had kettle corn?
- Escalators or elevators? Go!
- If I was a twin, would you like me more or less?
- Did you know that grapes explode in the microwave?
- How many times have you been to *Medieval Times*?
- Did you know some people feel the film *Forrest Gump* is actually conservative Christian propaganda?
- Which would you rather have: hiccups that never end or a butt itch every time you hear a phone ring?
- Would you still be into me if I didn't have a bellybutton?

STEP 3: SMALL TALK

When communicating via text or email, you can take three hours to come up with the perfect response and the time lapse only helps to add mystery (except for that time you took three hours thinking of a sext response and once you finally sent it, it was completely out of context). Time is not your friend when it comes to in-person conversations. Just remember the golden rule: Everyone is a narcissist and loves to talk about themselves. Ask him a ton of questions and he'll feel an instant connection with you.

As a backup: If it turns out you have nothing in common and the hour is late, just stick your tongue in his mouth. Then everyone wins and the evening isn't a total wash.

STEP 4: NUMBER SWAP

It's time to exchange digits. Don't be afraid to ask for his name again if you didn't catch it the first time, otherwise you'll wind up super excited for your date with "Mr. Widowspeak Glasses Red Shirt Jägerbomb, MD." However, it is important that you include a descriptive nickname in the "notes" section of the contact (the geniuses at Apple didn't put that category in for no reason). If you're going to be asking friends for advice post–number swap, the last thing you want is a mix-up. Your friends won't remember which guy "Brian" was, but they most certainly will remember Doctor Jägerbomb. Specificity is essential.

SUGGESTED NICKNAMES

Note: Feel free to borrow, steal, or adjust as needed to keep track of your Rolodex of Romeos. Alternatively, most of these also work as names for bars.

- Bearded Mahogany
- The One with a Girly Dog
- Grandpa Hands
- High School Jesus
- Whiny Penthouse
- Good on Paper
- Mustached Bearcub
- The Non-Mormon Mormon
- Baldwin Brother
- Hairy Honey Badger
- The Curved Frenchie
- Orgasmic Napoleon
- Smelly Bikram
- Sad Resting Face
- Little Dutch Boy
- Artisanal Sweaterhead
- Black-Tie Ball Sack
- Head of Dome
- Midnight Wailer
- Disproportionate Baby Head

MORAL OF THE STORY

THE BATTLE IS NOT ALWAYS WON BY YOUR PHONE

While it's tempting to want to hide behind your phone instead of taking a risk and engaging with a real-life guy, just think, a little bravery at a bar can lead to a night filled with secrets revealed, souls bared, and a new Facebook friend (What? No! Don't add him already!). If things go even better than expected, you might be upstairs in the apartment of a flesh-and-blood human male, huddled over his bathroom sink shaving your legs with his Gillette while muttering to yourself, "Why didn't I shave my legs tonight?" and "I promised myself I wouldn't hook up with a guy I just met. Why do I do this? Every time. Every fucking time. Go home now. I should just leave." Good luck with that.

TIWYS

You're Looking for Guys in All the Wrong Places

The Incidents and the Club

INCIDENT REPORT 1	
1. DATE 11/05/2015	**4. INJURY TYPE** "Literally making my eardrums bleed!"
2. TIME 9:03 P.M.	
3. LOCATION Goldbar, New York City	

5. DETAILS OF INCIDENT
Patient was positioned among a crowd of partygoers corralled behind the velvet rope outside of the premises. A male (Subject 1) approached Patient, pinched her waist, and said, "Ride 'em, cowgirl." Patient was not wearing any cowgirl paraphernalia. Patient's eardrums immediately began to bleed profusely.

6. FIRST AID ADMINISTERED
The bouncers yelled to the DJ to turn up the music inside to drown out the sound of Subject 1's voice. Patient could hear nothing but Icona Pop's "I Love It" and the hemorrhaging ceased.

INCIDENT REPORT 2

1. DATE
11/05/2015

4. INJURY TYPE
"Literally ripping my eyeballs out!"

2. TIME
11:24 P.M.

3. LOCATION
Goldbar, New York City

5. DETAILS OF INCIDENT
Patient was positioned on the dance floor when a male (Subject 2) approached her. Although still unable to hear over the Swedish electro-pop, patient enjoyed a lip-reading conversation with Subject 2 and reported that he seemed like he "had it going on." When Patient turned away to set her drink down on a table, she turned back around and witnessed Subject 2 grinding on the dance floor with a petite, platinum blond Asian woman, engaging in what Patient described as "basically dry humping and I'm pretty sure I saw a hand go inside her." Patient instinctively ripped out her own eyeballs.

6. FIRST AID ADMINISTERED
A bartender informed Patient that she would not be served unless she put her eyes back in their sockets and offered her seltzer water and a white bar napkin to cleanse the open wound. After an entire student body of underage prep-school kids were let in, the coat check line grew deep enough to spill out onto the dance floor, obscuring the view of Subject 2 and the petite Asian blond, allowing Patient to keep her eyeballs in their sockets.

INCIDENT REPORT 3

1. DATE
11/06/2015

2. TIME
2:17 A.M.

3. LOCATION
Goldbar, New York City

4. INJURY TYPE
"Literally killing my soul!"

5. DETAILS OF INCIDENT
Patient reunited with her group of friends, who had joined three men at a corner booth in exchange for portions of the Grey Goose bottle service they had purchased. One of the men (Subject 3) introduced himself, not by name, but by stating, "Hi, I'm John Mayer's tour manager" and continued to spend the next forty-five minutes talking about John Mayer. Upon examination, tests show Patient's soul left the body around the 32-minute mark.

6. FIRST AID ADMINISTERED
Goldbar's manager requested emergency services in the form of an UberX car, while roommates were able to reattach the soul after a thirteen-hour emergency procedure that involved binge-watching the first season of The Mindy Project and cheesy fries from the 24-hour diner, followed by a three-day juice cleanse. Rehabilitation recommended: avoiding clubs. ●

WHERE TO GO

If you hear the words cover, celebrity appearance, guest DJ, or promoter, get ready for a night of teens tripping on Molly, Lucky Charms–flavored Smirnoff vodka spilled on your dress, and hair extensions stuck to the bottom of your shoes. This scene is great for bachelorette parties, birthday parties, practicing that new dance move you stole from eight-year-old twins while hate-watching *America's Got Talent*, and nights when you feel like making some bad decisions. But if you're looking for something lasting, it's probably not gonna happen here.

The foundation of any good relationship is the ability to carry on a conversation and continually discover new things that you enjoy about that person. So if your first meeting occurs in a locale where you can barely hear yourself think, let alone hear another person say "hello," you are not off to a great start.

While you wouldn't think there would be such a huge gap between the type of men who frequent clubs and the type you meet at bars, you would be wrong. Drinking a brew and playing darts with a group of buddies or sipping a house red during happy hour is a vastly different atmosphere from strobe lights and "go-go dancers" on poles. Granted, you could very well meet a loser at a bar, but the ability to identify said loser will come much faster if you can at least hear the losery things he's saying.

MORAL OF THE STORY

GUYS ARE WHERE THEY DRINK

Choose quality over quantity. There might be a lot of guys at a club, but just know that no guy ever spends $1,500 on bottle service, buys tickets to see Calvin Harris, or goes anywhere in Las Vegas with the intention of meeting a nice girl to bring home to mom.

Instead of going to places you think will have a large volume of men, choose places you think will have the type of men you want to meet. You're more likely to find compatibility when you do things that you enjoy. Dig kale? Join a community garden. Need an audience for your haiku? Go to an open mic. Wish you were better at running on sand? Join a volleyball league. You'll have way more in common than just a mutual affinity for paying for watered-down drinks.

PICK-UP LINES FOR ANY LOCATION

- The Apple Store: "I have some files I would love to back up into your hard drive."
- Archery Class: "You must be an arrow . . . because if you were inside me? It would make me *quiver*."
- Wine Club: "I like my men like I like my Cabernet Sauvignon: full-bodied, but firm with a hint of acidity."
- Whole Foods: "These honeydews are GMO-free."
- Dog Adoption Center: "I'm totally against breeding—unless it's between humans."
- Game Night: "You don't have a *Clue* what kind of *Trouble* we could get into if you take a *Risk* and put your hands on my *Hungry Hungry Hippos* and your *Battleship* inside my *Yahtzee*."
- Improv Class: "How about we get a little Del *Closer*? I'll be yelling 'Yes and' all night long."
- Yacht Club: "If you need help hoisting your sail, I promise my luff is tight."
- Cooking Class: "I think I'm an apron because I should be on you."
- Glass-Blowing Class: Any blowing reference works here.

IT'S TECHY

53

Text Messages Are Confusing

The Friends and the Phone

You've spent the last few years preparing for the ping-pong game of witty banter, well-placed punctuation, and ironic-to-genuine emoji use you expect to engage in when you meet the man of your dreams. But now you have a problem. You've met that man. You've been chatting back and forth with him and you really thought it was going somewhere. But today is your birthday and he has stood you up. You are upset. You are confused. You don't understand. You run to your most trusted friend, who has declared herself to be the expert decipherer of the confusing code that is your mobile love affair.

You say things like: "Do you think Tommy likes me?" and "Why isn't he coming?"

Your friend, Mallory, also known as your digital-dick-soothsayer, pulls out her metaphorical magnifying glass and sets out to get to the real answers hidden here. As with many forms of written communication, so much is up to interpretation. She is a strong interpreter. She has spent years sifting through all of this nonsense, reading between the lines and figuring out what a guy is *really* trying to say by that "hey." he sent you at exactly 3:46 P.M. It has become a real art.

You know she will have the answers for you today.

"Men are just confusing creatures, but I know what they really mean," Mallory informs you. "You are interpreting this all wrong!"

Tommy

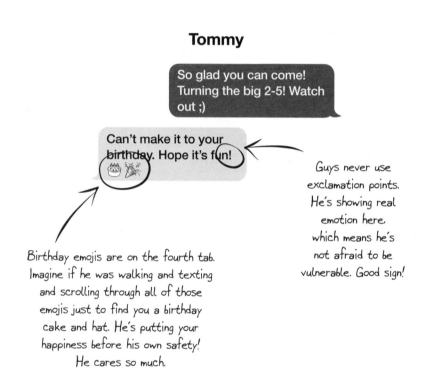

> So glad you can come! Turning the big 2-5! Watch out ;)

> Can't make it to your birthday. Hope it's fun! 🎂 🎉

Guys never use exclamation points. He's showing real emotion here, which means he's not afraid to be vulnerable. Good sign!

Birthday emojis are on the fourth tab. Imagine if he was walking and texting and scrolling through all of those emojis just to find you a birthday cake and hat. He's putting your happiness before his own safety! He cares so much.

"Really?" you ask, after surveying her notes. You're unsure whether to believe your friend's well-researched and clearly fact-based theory. "Cause, I mean, it's my birthday. The day I was born. I just always thought that if a guy really liked you, he'd send flowers or come to your birthday dinner."

She rolls her eyes and insists you are never grateful for anything, not even grateful for a man taking the time to send *two* birthday emojis.

You wish you could just call Tommy and ask him what was up—no need to interpret tone or intention. But you know better. Text messages are quick, easy, and impersonal, three things very appealing to members of your generation.

Mallory is happy to prove her expertise once again by offering up some more analysis on a text Tommy sent you two nights ago.

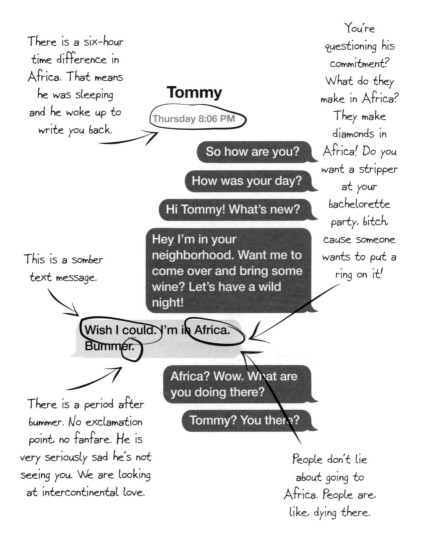

There is a six-hour time difference in Africa. That means he was sleeping and he woke up to write you back.

You're questioning his commitment? What do they make in Africa? They make diamonds in Africa! Do you want a stripper at your bachelorette party, bitch, cause someone wants to put a ring on it!

Tommy

Thursday 8:06 PM

So how are you?

How was your day?

Hi Tommy! What's new?

Hey I'm in your neighborhood. Want me to come over and bring some wine? Let's have a wild night!

This is a somber text message.

Wish I could. I'm in Africa. Bummer.

Africa? Wow. What are you doing there?

Tommy? You there?

There is a period after bummer. No exclamation point, no fanfare. He is very seriously sad he's not seeing you. We are looking at intercontinental love.

People don't lie about going to Africa. People are like dying there.

"Are you sure?" you question. On one hand, of course you trust your friend. But on the other hand, she is in the same single boat as you and her last boyfriend was a sex addict she met when she bought a used fish tank on Craigslist. But your friend knows best, simply because she is your friend.

"Why so negative? What we have here is a classic case of low self-esteem," Mallory theorizes. "Are you unable to accept real love? What is your hang-up?" She says you don't deserve her precious time and energy. She is about to leave, but then she remembers a time when the roles were reversed and it was you staring into her poor, needy cow eyes and helping her through a complex mobile affair. It is her duty to guide you through this difficult time. She will stay. A blossoming love affair can make an unstable fool out of all of us. Mallory takes a look-see at one last text.

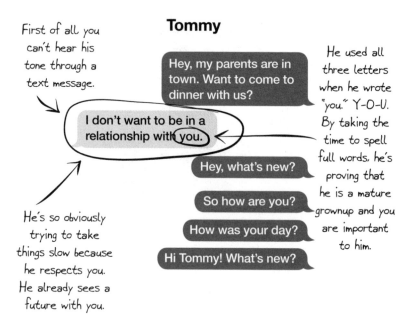

First of all you can't hear his tone through a text message.

Tommy

Hey, my parents are in town. Want to come to dinner with us?

I don't want to be in a relationship with you.

Hey, what's new?

So how are you?

How was your day?

Hi Tommy! What's new?

He used all three letters when he wrote "you." Y-O-U. By taking the time to spell full words, he's proving that he is a mature grownup and you are important to him.

He's so obviously trying to take things slow because he respects you. He already sees a future with you.

You start to go dizzy. You are very confused, but like a young Luke Skywalker, you have slowly been swayed away from the dark side of cynicism thanks to Mallory's Yoda-like wisdom. The Force is strong.

Now is the finale.

The fun part for your friend! The part Mallory has been waiting for this entire time. With the full understanding of the situation, she gets to both creatively and methodically concoct the perfect response to your guy. It's like being back in Civil War times when lovers had to express all their desires and yearning through the written word. It's also like when Mallory was in third grade and wrote a story about how she was actually a unicorn who lived in the clouds. It's just like both of those things. Basically, it's time to get creative. Romance is in the air, the possibilities are limitless, and she knows just what to write.

"The emojis were INCREDIBLY thoughtful," she begins, as you type furiously, following her instructions . . .

Tommy

The emojis were INCREDIBLY thoughtful. You always go above and beyond. I want you to know - I don't need you to travel the world to Africa to get me jewelry, i don't need you to wait until everything in your life is perfect. I am already your princess and you are my prince!

This is bad.

I hope you die.

"Don't worry, that probably wasn't literal," she assures you. "Still, I guess it wasn't meant to be."

You appear comatose.

"Also," she asserts, "pretty sure I didn't tell you to add that exclamation mark at the end. No offense, but that's probably where you went wrong. Too aggressive." ●

REMOVE THE LOVE GOGGLES

While it appears you have just turned your potential courtship into a romantic Hiroshima, it happens to the best of us. When you like a guy, love goggles cloud your rational brain, making you confused, not able to read the very clear signs, and in a desperate search for answers. It's easy to interpret everything wrong, look too hard at stuff that isn't there, or miss stuff that *is* there, when you're crushing hard.

Think about it: Text messages from other people in your life are usually not confusing to you. When's the last time you've asked for help analyzing a text message from your best friend, your Uber driver, or your mom? (Okay, we take back the part about your mom. Texts from your mom are most likely very confusing, but that has nothing to do with you overanalyzing and more to do with a combination of her bad eyesight, poor mastery of autocorrect, and attempt to sound young by sending you a rocket ship emoji instead of writing "good morning.")

MORAL OF THE STORY

I OVERTHINK, THEREFORE I AM SINGLE

This can all be remedied with a simple trick of the brain: Pretend he is your cousin. Unless you grew up in the Appalachians and this guy was your cousin all along, you'll be friendly, courteous, and when he doesn't text you back, you'll assume your "cousin" is either still in class or slammed with a busy day at the office and you'll wait for him to write you back. It's just a little expert substitution work!

Before you write a guy back, just ask yourself WWITC: "What Would I Text Cousin?" You won't be overly flirtatious to your cousin (because that's called incest) and that's good because guys don't want to date Gollum (we're talking about the desperate "We wants it. We needs it." aspect. But sure, they probably aren't into his looks either). You won't be overanalyzing the texts, because remember, *it's just your cousin*.

If you don't have a cousin, there are many other options to use: your boss, your neighbor, a classmate. The important thing is that you treat this new guy like he is just close enough to be polite to but in that distant kind of way that keeps him interested. Be nice, be your smart and funny self, but don't be desperate.

> **WARNING: This does not work for human-to-human contact. When you go on an actual date, DO NOT pretend he is your cousin. This could cause harmful psychological effects.**

You're a Stalker

The Detective and the Facebook

You walk into a dimly lit office in an alleyway to meet Agent McKinsy, an expert PI, who was highly rated on Yelp (and only $$ out of $$$$!). It's like you've suddenly stepped into the world of an old film noir. Smoke billows around his desk (from an e-cigarette, naturally), jazzy saxophone music blares (from an *L.A. Noire* playlist on Spotify), and he's adorned in a trench coat and fedora (sure, he's a modern-day agent, but Humphrey Bogart is still his style icon).

"The name's McKinsy, Private Eye, Undercover Investigator and Social Media Specialist," he states authoritatively. He stares at you from across his desk, cluttered with various tech gadgets, and continues. "There she was. A gorgeous dame in a dress so tight it looked like she'd been poured into it. What strange fate has brought her here?"

You explain you have a last-minute date and you need to know everything he can dig up.

"I met him last week at a dive bar in Brooklyn. His name is James. He had brownish hair, well it was kind of a dirty blond. He said he went to school for business. That's all I know."

Agent McKinsy types furiously at his computer. He flips it around.

"James Bradford. Cornell University."

"Oh my god—that's him!"

"Private eyes are trained to read between the lines. And search Facebook. His profile pic is him and a beagle."

"What?" you gasp. "He told me he didn't have any pets. That liar!"

"Well, if it was his dog, that'd be more of an Instagram thing so it's got to be the roommate's. Technically *not* his dog," he reveals. "If I had to guess, roommate got the dog but quickly lost interest. It became James's responsibility and now he wants to move out of the apartment but he loves the dog too much . . . This means he isn't good with confrontation."

"Passive-aggressive tendencies," you conclude.

This is worth every penny.

"I'm going to check all of the usual suspects: Facebook, Instagram, YouTube, Twitter, LinkedIn, Snapchat, Gchat away message, Tumblr, Foursquare, Venmo, Goodreads, Pinterest, SoundCloud, Amazon Wish List, Google Plus, Flickr, and Vines of James and all of his ex-girlfriends, best friends, co-workers, family, and anyone he might have interacted with in the last week."

"Geez, that sounds exhausting," you marvel, as you lean in closer. "Keeping up with someone's social media sounds like a full-time job."

"How do you think I make my rent, sister?" Agent McKinsy quips, as he simultaneously types on his laptop, desktop, iPad, iPhone, and some weird Tom Cruise in *Minority Report*–style hologram device. "Look! Him with a blond. He has his arm wrapped around her waist."

"He has a girlfriend? That motherfucker!"

"The blond is five years old. His niece. He enjoys being an uncle . . . But this is still bad."

"Oh, I know," you say, as you roll your eyes. "It means he's probably with his family, like, all of the time."

"Bingo. You can't imagine some of the grisly stuff I've witnessed in this line of work. I've seen the seedy underbelly of social media; you just don't know a person until you find their Facebook account, or worse . . . Pinterest."

He has a Pinterest? You don't believe it.

"Say it ain't so!" you howl. "The only people who actually use Pinterest are brides getting married or old ladies looking for a good chicken pot pie recipe. What sort of stuff is on there?"

"Photos of dead bodies, knives, chainsaws, wooden sheds, duffle bags," he lists.

Holy shit. You were about to be murdered.

"Actually, it appears James is throwing a *Walking Dead* premiere party next week," Agent McKinsy says. "He's one of those *theme party* guys."

You'll have to search deep in your soul to see if you can let this one slide.

"Jackpot!" Agent McKinsy exclaims. "Just found his Instagram account. It's a photo of him in front of the New York City skyline. He used a Sutro filter—the darkest and most suicidal filter of all. You can't trust a man who uses Sutro, Kelvin, or Lo-Fi."

Before you can tell Agent McKinsy this is enough information, he blurts out—

"Gold mine! His Venmo account. He uses the app to transfer money he owes people. This week he paid a forty-seven-year-old known felon sixteen hundred dollars."

He pauses and squints at the screen.

"Oh wait, he was actually just paying rent. His landlord's been in and out of the system. James's record appears to be clear, but . . . "

You don't need to hear anymore. You already know too much.

Sure, James seems like an innocent social media-using guy, but you can't date a passive-aggressive, theme-party-throwing, Sutro-filtering psychopath. No siree. You thank Agent McKinsy for his thorough investigative work and immediately text James to cancel the date.

Five years later . . .

You're at a dinner party in a gorgeous loft in the Upper West Side. The hostess comes up to you.

"I don't think you've met my husband . . . James Bradford."

Dun. Dun. DUN.

He's a father of two, thoughtful uncle, nonjudgmental tenant, dog lover, and dedicated husband, who has outgrown his proclivity for theme parties. The things that could have been. ●

NOT-SO-INNOCENT BACKGROUND CHECKS

We are all stalkers. It's just the nature of the curious beast. One second, you're casually checking to see if you and a guy have any mutual friends on Facebook, and the next thing you know you've connected with his mom on LinkedIn. It's not your fault. There is so much information out there and you'd be an idiot not to look at it, right? This mama is not about to be catfished. Oh hell no!

Your parents didn't think geography was all you were learning about from Carmen Sandiego, did they? Instead of studying the topography of Kathmandu, you were really discovering how to search for clues by any means necessary.

If one day your dead body gets washed up in a river somewhere, with the fingerprints of that new guy you started dating all over you, it's going to be your fault if you never did a brief Google search and discovered that YouTube video of his Nickelback cover band performing at a brony convention. You would have run for your life weeks before your gruesome death!

All of this stalkery is not limited to simply searching the web. There is a reason why when you hear about a "drive-by" on the news, you just assume it involves a girl in an idling car and her potential boyfriend's apartment. But generally, actual stalkery and the dangers that come with it (someone seeing you) are largely avoidable, thanks to location-based apps that easily give you his whereabouts (just remember to clear your browser history).

There might be a time when you meet a guy and you're not sure if he looks familiar because he went to college with you, he's on a TV show you watch, or he's a friend of a friend of a friend of a guy you went out with once. The problem is that sometimes web searches are like getting lost in the streets of Paris. You start wandering around the 5th *arrondissement* and the next thing you know you've made six rights, thirteen lefts, and you're contributing to a Kickstarter for an underwater microwave invented by the cousin of a guy you're going out with. It happens.

MORAL OF THE STORY — CURIOSITY KILLED THE COUPLE

You should make a moderate search of the web before a date, like making sure he isn't on any "Most Wanted" lists, the long-term ex-boyfriend of a friend, or worse—there is absolutely no information about him. If that happens, delete his number and block him immediately. You might have your very own Frank Abagnale Jr. on your hands (see Leonardo DiCaprio's disappearing con-artist character in the film *Catch Me If You Can*). But searching every nook and cranny of the web for information on a guy you're going out with is not necessary.

You can't judge the complexities of a human being by the amalgamation of his social media profiles (unless he is posting gratuitous, shaky, sweaty Vines of himself bench-pressing at the gym. Gross.). And digging too deep will just make you look creepy. You might not even realize you're doing it until you reflexively suggest on a first date, "Do you want to get dessert? They have peach cobbler and isn't that your favorite?" When your date gives you a confused "How did you know?" stare, do you really want to fess up to the fact that you saw his mom's Facebook post—"Making my son's favorite dessert, peach cobbler"—from over a year ago? Learn too much about him the old-fashioned way. Talking.

AGENT MCKINSY'S GUIDE TO PASSWORDS

Guys Who Are Keepers

- 1700583*
- mRcOMMitmenT1
- mONOgamY99
- 2cool2bcheating
- bUyUaPuppy

Guys Who Are Creepers

- StaCie4ever**
- 8Heroin8
- bAllSaCK696969
- oLDsp1cE4Life
- il1umnatlZhawt

*This is his yearly income.
**This is only bad if your name is not Stacie.

Ur Txts R Ridic

The Teen and the Texts

No matter how we are communicating, one rule has become the law of the land: Get to the point. You, however, just got out of a long-term relationship and are unfamiliar with this relatively recent protocol.

When you were in a relationship, you could send your boyfriend a three-paragraph text and actually continue to hear from him. Well, sister, now you're single and no one cares what you have to say. At least if it's longer than a few sentences.

You need help. You need a translator or an informant, someone who speaks this new language of love and can give you the most up-to-date information on how to navigate the unfamiliar landscape of brevity and carelessness.

You turn to Harper, the thirteen-year-old who lives two houses down.

She gives you a meeting location and a few demands. Information doesn't come cheap, and the risk of being seen in public with an old chatterbox like you is too high.

You show up at the secret location: the Frederick's of Hollywood at your local mall. She's so busy shoplifting lace thongs with one hand and texting with the other, that she almost doesn't notice you.

"I brought the stuff," you whisper.

You hand Harper a manila envelope. She discreetly peeks inside.

"One Direction at Madison Square Garden. Row H," she reads. "Not bad. Guess this is worth a lot to you."

"My life depends on it," you tell her candidly.

"Let me level with you," she begins, as she picks at her intricate nail art. "The days of beautiful prose and poetry are over. If bae wants to be sweet, you'll be lucky if he sends you a smile emoji blowing a heart out of its mouth. Keep it short and sweet. And whenever possible, god forbid, do not use full words."

"Ok, but—"

"Bitch! Do not look directly at me. I don't want people to know we are together. Jesus."

You awkwardly pick up some crotchless panties and pretend to examine them while she begins to school you on her theory of evolutionary linguistics.

"It's simple cultural progression," she lectures. "The evolution of language parallels the growth of technological achievements that have allowed us to multitask at a rate like never before. We have become a culture appreciative of those who are considerate enough not to waste our precious time with trivial things. Like full words. Following Darwin's theory of evolution, those who can't adapt become victims of singlehood."

"I had no idea," you marvel. "Are words going to become obsolete?"

"It's possible," she says. "Look, I'm only in eighth grade and I'm sure you were expecting some conventionalized clichéd version of a thirteen-year-old, right? But here I am with the vocabulary of someone twice my age. It's the Internet, brah. You can learn anything. But just because I have an impressive lexicon in my arsenal, doesn't mean I'm gonna use it."

A few days later you meet a cute guy named Nate. You refuse to be a victim of natural selection. Time to put your new acronym skills to use.

Nate

Hey u almost out of work?

Basically in the clear homey ———→ BITCH

Whoa, what's your problem?

Beats the heck out of me ———→ BTHOOM

Oh uh...sorry to interrupt. Tummy ache?

How are you ————————→ HAY

Um hi.

HAY

hi

By the tenth "hi." from Nate you realize what's going on, but it's too late—he thinks you're either a sociopath or just an asshole.

Back to Frederick's you go.

"What are those acronyms!?" Harper asks, as she glares at you with disdain. "I was talking about your everyday STFU, IMO, WTF, LMK, IDGAF. Being an old bag is no excuse for not doing this shit correctly."

"I can't even remember all of those two-letter words that get you the extra points in Scrabble," you cry. "How am I supposed to remember what acronyms are popular?"

"Look, lately I've been feeling acronyms are so passé anyways."

You stare at her. "Passé? I just saw you two days ago."

"One day you're trending, the next you're not," Harper huffs, as she tosses her blue-tipped hair. "Try abbreviations. Amaze, ridic, def, perf!"

You thank her and slip her a bag containing the Invisalign retainer she requested as payment.

After a date with Hunter, a new guy you met online, you give abbreviations a shot.

Hunter

I had a great time on our date last night.

amazing ⟶ Amaze

A maze? Oh, sorry if I was puzzling you... How was the rest of your night?

gorgeous ⟶ Gorge

Ate a lot of food, eh? That's uh, cool. What ya up to later?

getting cocktails ⟶ Getting cocks

I dig a girl who's open about her sexuality.

You schedule another meeting with your informant.

"You have straight teeth because of me, motherfucker!" you yell.

A stripper nearby browsing nippless bras in Frederick's gasps as you pull your informant into the dressing room.

"What are you doing?" she scolds. "I didn't say *only* text in abbreviations! You noob. You are so dumb!"

Harper takes a breath and begins scrolling through her phone covered in its gaudy Chanel case.

"I'm sorry," she calmly tells you. "It's been a really rough week for me. My friend Sophie got her 100,000th Tumblr follower before I did . . . Try emojis instead, 'k?"

She taps her foot, awaiting payment.

"Be careful with these," you say as you pull out a small box of Trojans. You hesitate as you look at the young teen.

"Ewww. Who am I, Juno? I have far too promising a future to complicate things with a teen pregnancy. I've only just begun to grasp the ramifications of my sexuality," she says. "I'm putting these on that bitch Sophie's lawn when my friends and I go toilet-papering tonight."

When a handsome friend of a friend named Liam gets in touch with you, you give Harper's advice one last shot.

Liam

Hope u don't mind I got ur number from a friend.

It was a gamble texting u

I already feel a spark too

It feels a little soon to talk about kids...

Huh?

If only cry face emojis had runny mascara to more accurately capture the emotion you feel after this conversation. ●

TALKING LIKE TWEENS

The economy of language may be your justification for communicating like a thirteen-year-old panty-stealing, info-sharing, future employee of the CIA, but overuse these tactics and people will start to wonder if your spelling is really so bad that even your iPhone can't autocorrect you. Too many laughing tongue-face emojis, "hilar!s", or "LOLs" and your cover is blown—no one really laughs *that* much. You're a grown-ass intelligent woman with too many college degrees; don't let tweens bully you into their ways!

Sure, it's funny to send your friend the peach emoji when she is talking about going up a pant size because that emoji looks like a butt. However, what would be even more helpful are fully formed words about how she is beautiful at any size and how Nicki Minaj has made an entire career out of that.

It was one thing when the one-word texts you were getting from guys made it feel like dating Lil Jon ("yeah," "what," "okay"), but then you took it to the next level by essentially cutting words in half ("whatevs," "obvs," "brill"). Even Cher in *Clueless* had the wherewithal to say the entirety of the word "whatever"!

MORAL OF THE STORY **LESS IS SOMETIMES NOT ENOUGH**

There is no need to completely ban abbreviations from your life. But it's important to know when they're appropriate, when your texts have become completely incomprehensible, and when you just sound, well, kind of dumb. It's fine to shorten things every now and then, as long as you don't go overboard. Like the saying goes: Use in moderation.

A good rule of thumb: If a phrase or word is more of an effort to abbreviate than to write out, you probably shouldn't do it. At some point, you'll need to have a real conversation with this person, so why get into the habit of restricting your vocab? Uh, vocabulary.

EMOJI ETIQUETTE 101

 OK: It's so cold outside.
NOT OK: More conflict in the Middle East.

 OK: I think I failed my algebra exam.
NOT OK: Grandpa died.

 OK: I got a raise.
NOT OK: Grandpa died.

 OK: Can't wait for our girls' night.
NOT OK: I think my daughter is a lesbian.

 OK: Need Tylenol. Bad headache.
NOT OK: Sorry about your brother's overdose.

 OK: You looked hot tonight.
NOT OK: Help! My house is on fire.

TIWYS

You're Insta-Dating

The Man Dolls and the Shopper

When you finally decide to go to Onely, the store that everyone you know is shopping at except for you, you can't believe it took you so long. The place is magnificent and sprawling, with aisle upon aisle of different Man Dolls, each enclosed in an individual glass case of the same size (7' tall, 3' wide, and 3' deep). There are dolls of every age, clothing style, haircut, eye color, nose shape, and skin tone imaginable, all lined up in organized rows. The interior decor at Onely is minimal, with muted colors and no artwork on the walls or fancy displays in the floor-to-ceiling windows. Onely has stripped away the excess and kept only what is necessary.

"It all looks so simple," you say out loud, as you look around in wonder.

The challenges of trying to find a Man Doll before Onely opened were time-consuming and unreliable. You never knew where to find a doll you wanted in stock. Friends would recommend dolls but you never liked them. Sometimes a Man Doll would be displayed in a window, but when you would inquire about purchasing it, you would find out that the doll was, in fact, not actually for sale. But every Man Doll in Onely is for sale. It is a convenient, one-stop shop.

You walk down the aisle marked "22–34" and glide your finger across the glass box of a Man Doll labeled Elliot. You read the box, which lists just a few facts. Elliot was manufactured in Park Slope, is twenty-seven years old, and is part of the limited edition "Filmmaker" line. You roll your eyes and lean in close to get a better look at Elliot, with his slouched beanie and flannel shirt. "Limited edition, my ass," you whisper under your breath. "This is just a repackaged Unemployed Man Doll."

You keep walking and pass a Sexy Nerd Man Doll labeled Davy, a Freelance Man Doll labeled Scott, and a Party Boy Man Doll labeled Luke. The smile on the Party Boy line of dolls is so engaging. You are instantly drawn to it, but a voice in your head reminds you this is a bad idea.

You previously owned a Party Boy Man Doll labeled Logan. The doll had been traded in by someone who was tired of it and you were duped by the enthusiastic salesman at the second-hand store.

"Logan will be the life of the party," the sales clerk told you, noting that the box promised "endless energy."

A couple months later, you realized the doll needed Adderall in order to function properly. You hadn't read the disclaimer carefully enough. The returns department was a huge hassle and the entire process got drawn out another month, with you almost deciding to keep Logan but then going through with the return after all. "Don't make the same mistake again," you chant to yourself, reminded of your horrible buyer's remorse.

You walk further down the aisle and stop at a dark-eyed Intellectual Man Doll labeled Julian. It was manufactured in Westchester County and is holding a Harvard diploma in its left hand. You lift up the paper flap on the label to read more information. "Like a good brew, love a good book, need a good girl." Just as you are sure you have decided on Julian, you spot a doll labeled Logan next to it. Oh my god. It's *your* Logan. Well, your ex-doll. The one you returned.

"Fuck!" you shout as you duck down. "Shit, shit, fuck."

You crawl down the aisle on all fours. "It's not even fucking activated," you remind yourself. Still, you can feel Logan's frozen eyes burning into the back of your head. "Of course, Logan gets refurbished *after* I return it," you mutter, as you finally lift yourself up once you're out of eyeline.

You continue down the aisle. You write down the SKU numbers for a chiseled Sporty Man Doll labeled Ty, a blond-haired Entrepreneur Man Doll labeled Cooper, and a kind-eyed Boy Next Door Man Doll labeled Corey.

A pounding headache begins pulsing in the back of your skull. The overabundance of choices is starting to feel more taxing than helpful. Relieved to have reached the end of the aisle, you turn the corner, expecting to see a checkout counter.

You gasp.

There are hundreds more aisles, just like the one you spent the last four hours shopping in, all marked 22–34. Thousands of glass cases, some stacked on top of one another, line the aisles. You see now that the store is ten times larger than any Costco warehouse you've been in, all filled with Man Dolls.

You have barely scratched the surface.

You feel dizzy and begin running down the aisle. It doesn't end. The dolls, which can last a lifetime if you choose the right one or a couple days if you choose a faulty one, all begin to look indistinguishable from one another. You are angry at this uncurated marketplace of dolls that claimed to be a simpler way to shop.

You will never be able to view them all.

You close your eyes, and blindly choose a doll on the shelf. You grip the large brass handle on the side of the case and with all of your force, you hoist it off the shelf and drag it toward the front of the store. Your cheeks are flushed, your eyes bloodshot, and sweat glistens off your forehead.

"How can I help you?" says the woman behind the counter.

"I'd like . . . to purchase . . . this Man Doll," you pant, out of breath.

She scans the barcode.

"Oh, dear. I'm sorry, but it looks like this Man Doll is reserved."

"What?" you shout. "I thought all Man Dolls at Onely are available!"

"They are," she says. "But it looks like another customer snatched it up just minutes before you."

"But I didn't even see any other customers. I thought I was the only one in the store."

"Yeah, it's designed that way. It's better for everyone. I can add your name to the wait list in case it's returned?"

You shake your head no, knowing better than to waste your time waiting around for a doll that might never be returned. You take a deep breath and compose yourself.

You turn around, and walk back toward aisle 22–34. ●

SWIPING THROUGH THE POPULATION

In the very palm of your hand lies an endless whirlpool of dating possibilities. Whether it's Tinder, OkCupid, Bumble, Match, eHarmony, Happn, Hinge, Grindr, Coffee Meets Bagel, Zoosk, PlentyOfFish, JSwipe, Badoo, Grouper, At First Sight, How About We, or some of the more recent copycat apps on the market like Spinster, MaybeAphrodite, Stumble, Rematch, aLarming, Nappn, Cringe, Humpr, Hot Dog Meets Bun, We Bought A Zoosk, FishInA-Barrel, BaeSwipe, DooDoo, ThirdWheeler, At Second Glance, How About We Fuck . . . it's hard to keep up.

You can stand in line at the post office and assume you've swiped your way through half the population in under twenty minutes. However, just when you think you've reached the end, an entirely new crop of faces, height specifications, and song quotes (there are a whole lot of men looking for women who like piña coladas and getting caught in the rain) pop up onto your screen. These profiles are like Mogwais from the movie *Gremlins*—except they don't need water to multiply, just your stress. What if the perfect guy is one swipe away?

You need to break this pattern of hyperconsumption. Just because there are twenty pages of dresses on NastyGal.com doesn't mean you need to order them all. But what if your dream dress is on the next page? Next. Next. By the time you reach the final page, you have a shopping cart full of dozens of ensembles that you'll never have the time to wear. (And seriously, were you drunk when you picked out those macramé leggings?)

MORAL OF THE STORY IF YOU'RE THE JACK OF ALL SWIPES, YOU'LL BE A MASTER OF NONE

You're not giving a relationship a chance when you insta-date.

Sure, it's wise not to invest *too* much in a first date before you know things are going somewhere. But if you invest absolutely nothing in anyone, then you might as well have stayed home and watched a compilation of Vines of cats knocking things over.

Stop looking over your date's shoulder for the next best thing. Yes, it's distracting when you innocently check the time on your phone and spy a dating app notification beckoning you. But that "chill dude" from Astoria who wants to know "how your night is going" can probably wait for you to answer him about setting up a new date when you get home from your current date. You'll never notice the endearing way this one pulls at his collar or the way he smiles when you tell a story if you're staring at the phone sitting in your crotch. That new-age friend of yours that's always talking about her spirit animal is on to something: Stay in the moment.

Man Dolls

COLLECT AND TRADE WITH FRIENDS!

Boy Next Door MAN DOLL

Searching for the perfect mom for my sweet Labrador Rufus.

World Traveler MAN DOLL

Nicaragua, Israel, France, Dubai, Greece, India, Sudan, Russia, China. Citizen of the world. Love charity work and blonds above 5'5".

Party Boy MAN DOLL

Cîroc, Prosecco & Champagne, 420, Musica, Brunch, Real Estate, Everywhere, VIP, Art, Work hard, play hard.

Hipster MAN DOLL

Likes: Girls with bangs, vegan food, homebrews.

Artsy MAN DOLL

Check out my portfolio on IG #nofilter.

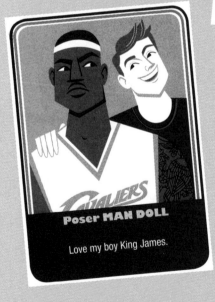

Poser MAN DOLL

Love my boy King James.

Sarcastic MAN DOLL

Looking for a girl with a terrible personality and no sense of humor.

Can't Come Up With His Own Jokes MAN DOLL

I have many leather-bound books and my apartment smells of rich mahogany.

Smooth-Talker MAN DOLL

I have a queen-size bed. I don't know any queens but if one came over, man she'd be comfortable.

Communication-Inept MAN DOLL

Needs a Therapist MAN DOLL

I don't know what people talk about on dates. I need someone who will listen. And talk me down. But mostly listen.

Humblebrag MAN DOLL

Just finished my PhD so I finally have time to go on dates.

Knows What You're Wondering MAN DOLL

I'm taller than you.

TIWYS

You Avoid Conflict

The Cave Woman and the Cave Guy

It's the early Stone Age in the year 500,000 BP. Your bombshell great-grandma[13], Cave Lady, is on a first date with a member of her tribe. Things are going pretty well. Cave Guy's cave doesn't have too many bones lying around and he's cleared out a lot of the bats for their date night. He also made an effort by wearing a neatly pressed saber-toothed tiger loincloth and by bathing three weeks ago. But halfway through the date, she notices his cave is a bit chilly. Not wanting to seem "high maintenance," she considers the best way to let him know she is uncomfortable. She settles on some nonverbal cues, such as shivering and pulling a woolly mammoth skin over her shoulders. He doesn't get it.

He repeatedly asks her if she is okay. "Urgah?" She mumbles an unconvincing "Uup" and frowns. While Cave Guy goes out to pick up their take-out food (the nonpoisonous berries at this great new spot one mountain, twelve trees, and three bushes away) for their dinner, she decides to solve the problem herself. She creates the first manmade fire using two decorative sticks she found lying around the cave.

She's pretty proud of herself and she's warm. But as soon as she hears some rustling in the bushes, she puts the fire out. He's returning and she doesn't want him to think she was being "nosy" or messing with his stuff.

Unfortunately, because of her unwillingness to speak her mind, the control of fire didn't happen for another hundred thousand years, thereby delaying the progress of human evolution and expansion. But even worse, it ruins dinner.

Things get a little more complicated once this nice cave couple move in together. Tired of asking her man for the 1,000th time to pick up toilet paper on his way home from going out grunting with the boys and not wanting to start a fight, Cave Lady instead chooses to simply etch her message into a wall of their cave.

This is the original passive-aggressive Post-it Note. To avoid witnessing his reaction upon return, Cave Lady runs out to spear a boar, conveniently around the time she expects her guy will return home. Had she stuck around and had a conversation, she might have learned that it's not that her Cave Guy isn't listening when she asks that he stop and pick things up, he's just unsure about what type of leafy vegetation she prefers to use after going to the bathroom. By running out, Cave Lady has put a further strain on an already tense relationship.

Also, she got trampled by that boar. ●

CONFLICT FROM A DISTANCE

You are really just channeling your caveman ancestors leaving stick-figure drawings on cave walls, when you text your man a dozen rose emojis on your anniversary after the day has gone by with no gifts.

Both men and women are guilty of avoiding conflict for different reasons. Men are usually not the best communicators and ladies fear being labeled "needy," "a nag," or "a shrew." This is due to a history of oppression, the struggle for equality and women's rights, and fear of garnering a rep like Julia Stiles in *10 Things I Hate About You*.

On top of the instinct to want to keep disagreements at bay, it's never been easier to avoid conflict thanks to technological advancements. While these inventions have given us access to instant communication with anyone, anywhere (we wouldn't be surprised if Alexander Graham Bell was that crazy ex-boyfriend who created the telephone after running out of ways to stalk his lady love), they have also gifted us countless ways to elude each other. From a safe distance we can text, email, and DM our loved ones in order to address the most awkward and complex of issues ("Why are you not answering my text messages?!"). If Adam and Eve could have screened a call from God after that apple debacle, there is no doubt they would have.

MORAL OF THE STORY IF YOU CAN'T STAND THE HEAT, HAVE A HEART-TO-HEART ABOUT LOWERING THE TEMPERATURE

The answer here is to follow the fear. Sure, face-to-face conflict is terrifying because you might get yelled at (!) and you might have to yell (!), but this means of communication involves the benefit of both verbal and social cues. As a result, nothing can be lost in translation. That means no hinting, no ominous dot-dot-dots, just straight up talk. Instead of toilet paper drawings and question marks, just say, "Yo, bring toilet paper home or I will feel like you are not listening or respecting my needs." Your cave ancestors would be proud.

THE HISTORY OF AVOIDING TALKING IN PERSON

Smoke Signals

Used to gather your fellow tribe pals for a powwow, warn your peeps there was a grizzly in the hood, or tell your boo that she was no longer the Chero-key to your heart . . . smoke signals had many uses. Your relationship wasn't the only thing up in flames, know what we mean?

Letter Writing

The original appeal of letter writing was delivering bad news. If you didn't want to hear the other person's response, you were in luck: It would be a long time (even longer if your messenger got hit by the plague).

Telephone

In your bedroom filled with black lights, a lava lamp from Spencer's, and your green blow-up couch, you could crank-call the hottest guy in school under the guise of being the casting agent from *Legends of the Hidden Temple*. God, you were cool. Then caller ID ruined your life.

Pager

Doctors and drug dealers in the '90s and Alan from *The Hangover* franchise weren't the only people to carry a pager. Pagers were the precursors to text messages for teens, except that you could only speak in number codes. Some pages sent your heart aflutter (1*177155*400 meant "I miss you") while others were more ambiguous (121 meant "I need to talk to you"). The person had no way of responding, at least until they could make it to a pay phone.

Instant Message

An away message or a user profile filled with morose '90s song lyrics, a ton of asterisks and tildes, or an ominous, out-of-context line from a young adult novel was a much easier way of telling a boy you were sad he didn't love you back.

Emails

Emails were great if you wanted to pen a lengthy manifesto to your main squeeze, then click "Send" and pretend that none of it ever happened. Automated vacation responses were also a great way to lay low. What happens on the Internet stays on the Internet. Right?

Text Messages

Steve Jobs and the good people at Apple revolutionized the way we avoid awkward situations by taking texting to the next level in a post-BBM world. It went from something we used as a last resort ("Can't talk now, in a meeting!") to a supremely easy way to lie ("Can't talk now, in a meeting!"). And thus, using your phone for speaking has become obsolete.

Text Message
Today 7:20 PM

can't come to your party i was kidnapped by drug lords. so bummed :(

THE EXCEPTION: *FaceTime*

FaceTime is awful for avoiding conflict. You are zoomed in on the actual human being in real time. On one hand, it's great if the guy you're seeing is out of town and you're having the best hair day of your life. It's not so great if the person contacting you is someone you have intentionally chosen to be very far away from . . . or if you're having a bad hair day. For this reason, don't expect your new iPhone to have a hologram option.

TIWYS

You Don't Know How to Advertise Yourself

The Profile and the Ad Agency

You decide it is time to catch up with the rest of the world and set up an online dating profile. A profile is essentially an advertisement for yourself. But how are you supposed to come up with an ad that can make you stand out among some of the fiercest competition—thousands of other intelligent, beautiful, and interesting women? You didn't study marketing in college! You decide to enlist the help of the professionals and hire an ad agency—Olson & Gallagher.

Olson & Gallagher has sent three of the company's best minds: legendary creative director William Albright, head marketing officer Rebecca Kelly, and chief of technology Zipher Medina. William reaches out his palm and shakes your hand up and down vigorously three times. You can tell this is not his first rodeo. He's a middle-aged gentleman with a pressed suit. His gray hair is slicked back and he's carrying a briefcase, an easel, and a flipchart pad. This guy is old school.

"Let's jump right into it," William says briskly, as he pours himself a whiskey on the rocks. "The research from our focus groups all say the same thing: You are lacking in branding and identity. How do you make the customer feel? Who *are* you? Right now your message is mixed. We need an emotional narrative, one that makes men feel a connection to you. Nostalgia. Sentiment. Endearment. Picture this: A young man sits at his kitchen table on a winter day. It's snowing. Sunlight glistens off the snow like diamonds."

Your mouth is agape.

"The kitchen table is the only place this young man can sit together with his roommates. The couch is too small for the three of them. But his roommate Chris likes video games. His other roommate Kevin is ironing his shirt for work. And all this young man wants is to bond with his friends and eat breakfast. What if there was *something* that could bring everyone together? Away from the video games. Away from the ironing board. Away from all of the chaos. What if there was something he could share?"

"A box of Rice Krispies?" you ask.

He slams his hands on the table for dramatic effect.

"Did I say Snap, Crackle, and Pop? It's your profile! The young man has to read your 'about me' section out loud to his friends. They crowd around the computer and take turns reading. They have connected with each other . . . through you. But right now, you have no story."

"I know sales have been slow but I did get a message from a guy named Billy last week," you say defensively. "He was asking me all sorts of questions about myself."

"That was me," William unabashedly tells you, as he lights himself a cigarette. "That was the only way to research the product—by interacting with you like a potential customer. That is the level of commitment we have at Olson & Gallagher. When we worked with Volkswagen on the New Beetle in 1998, we drove the car. When we worked with Mattel in 1984, we played with Hot Wheels. When we worked with Playtex in 1977, we used the tampons."

You cringe at the thought.

William theatrically pulls back the first sheet on the flipboard to reveal a mockup of your proposed dating profile.

F / Straight / Single

Slogan
The kind of girl your dog will love!

About Me
War. Disease. Social unrest. In a time of great uncertainty and sadness, a time when we could all use a break and a smile, I am the girl who always puts change in the tip jar, waves at children on the bus, and dances until the lights come on.

Favorite Things
Puppies, the Super Bowl, carpentry, community service, empanadas, global awareness. I'd love to tell you about the time I experienced all of these things in one day.

What I'm Looking For
I pick up my cup of coffee and stroll out onto my veranda. There my husband sits awaiting our morning ritual that we have practiced since the day we met, forty-two years ago. I place my weather-beaten hand on his shoulder and he smiles warmly. This is family. This is love. This is what I'm looking for.

They can tell you aren't exactly impressed by the hyper-poetic narrative pitch, so Rebecca jumps in as William slumps into his seat. She's a slender blonde woman in a skintight navy Alexander Wang dress. She pulls a hot pink laptop out of her Chloé bag and hooks it up to the projector screen.

"Another route we can go is by focusing on your brand's credibility," she states. "How do we do that?"

"By listing what college I went to and my double major?" you guess.

"Wrong! Celebrities legitimize your brand. If you place your-self by important people, you seem important," she says, as she clicks to bring up her first slide.

Celebrities fill the screen.

"Frosted Flakes had Groucho Marx in the '50s," she drawls. "I Can't Believe It's Not Butter had Fabio in the '80s and '90s. Proactiv had Katy Perry in the teens . . . And who do you have?"

She clicks to the next slide. Dear god. It's a photo of the prom king you lost your virginity to. How did she even get this photo?

"I see here in your company profile you hooked up with popular kid Dillon Hansford in high school. For now, he will absolutely do. Just take a look at *this*!"

F / Straight / Single

Slogan
It girl of the moment, your girl for life.

About Me
I live for a catered affair, a feisty dialogue, and the flashing bulbs of the paparazzi. I'm a fun girl, but you shouldn't take my word for it . . .

"Our time spent together was on another level. This girl is spontaneous, original, the best of the best. Whether it was the Winter Formal after-party or a kegger at my parents' house, she was a class act all the way. I'd totally hook up with her again."
    —Dillon Hansford, *Prom King, McMillan High School*

Favorite Things
Shopping with my sorority friends, charity events with rich people, dating entrepreneurs, facials with Malia Obama (that's my cat, but she has a following on Instagram).

What I'm Looking For
A solid plus-one with a name designed for the VIP list.

"As you know, I've been in charge of some of the most successful viral campaigns of the last five years," says Rebecca, as she reapplies her lipgloss. "'The Most Slutty Girl In The World?' That was me. 'Got Bangs?' That was this girl. Flo from Progressive? It was all moi."

"That's very impressive," you say. "But I just don't think this celebrity endorsement route is, uh, me."

Rebecca composes herself, barely concealing her disappointment, and takes a seat.

Zipher stands up next. He is wearing a sweater vest and Coke-bottle glasses. He pulls up various charts and graphs on the screen.

"A third option is to focus purely on the numbers," he says. "According to the analytics I've run, your CTR—that's click-through rate—is in the low ten percent. Not good. First off, we need to improve your SEO. Words like 'quirky,' 'chill,' and 'fun' get listed so much, they are essentially meaningless non-specifics that will turn up thousands of other results along with yours."

"But I *am* quirky, chill, and fun," you meekly rationalize.

"Use bolder language. Buzzwords like 'normcore,' 'yuccie,' and 'lumbersexual' are getting a lot of hits right now. There is a lot of competition in the marketplace. You need to stand out!"

Zipher dims the lights for dramatic effect and clicks a button on his computer. Three Photoshopped versions of your profile photo appear: a sporty version of you holding a baseball bat, a hunting version of you holding a gun and decked out in camo, and a farmer girl version of you posed next to a red tractor.

"By using interest-tailored recognition profiling, we can target custom ads for each customer," he says, as he paces the room.

Zipher uploads the three photos to your dating profile and you watch the messages flood in by the hundreds from various sports enthusiasts, gun lovers, and Midwest farm boys.

"What we charge for CPM—that's cost per 1,000 impressions —is insignificant compared to what you are investing in: the studmuffin of your dreams."

"Um, is it possible for you to delete the photo of me with the gun?" you ask. "I'm kind of a pacifist, plus I'm pretty sure there are some harsh penalties for possession of an unregistered firearm."

He ignores you.

"You're probably wondering how we are able to target such specific demos. It's all about their search history. You tell us the demographic you're looking to reach and we can find them."

"I don't know, I guess I just want a guy who is kind, smart, relatively clean," you answer.

"Clean. So you want a neat freak? Perfect. Allow me to show you what some eligible bachelor who just searched for 'drop-off laundry service' will see pop up above his searches."

F / Straight / Single

Slogan
So fresh and so clean, clean!

About Me
Crisp mind, clean lifestyle. I'm great at compartmentalizing—business and pleasure, life and love, colors and whites.

Favorite Things
Fragrant meadows, a made bed, fresh linens, discount detergent, and a talking teddy bear.

What I'm Looking For
Someone unafraid to show me they care by not shrinking my blouses and taking the time to bundle my pairs of socks into little balls.

"We are paving the way for outside-of-the-box thinking in the digital age," says Zipher. "What side of history do you want to be on?"

This is a lot of information to process. You'll need some time to weigh your options. You give each member of the team a handshake, and see them to the door. As soon as they leave, you find yourself a nice roomy hermitage on Airbnb where you can live a solitary, monk-like life, call Time Warner to cancel your Internet service, and then immediately throw your computer out the window. ●

CREATING THE PERFECT PROFILE

DON'T PRETEND TO BE A SECRET AGENT

Whether you want to look at it this way or not, it's a dating application. Writing something like "message me to ask about my favorite movies" is no different than writing "ask me in the interview where I went to college" on a work resume. You are not adding an air of mystery; you are being annoying. Considering it takes the same amount of time to write "message me" as it does to write "*Empire Records*," you wind up looking lazy and uninterested. Either fill out the section or don't.

GIVE SPECIFICS

Ironically, it's hard to say, "I am a smart person" without sounding like a real idiot. Instead, if you break down the mathematical formulations of quantum mechanics people are more inclined to believe you. Don't actually get into quantum mechanics, but try a brief, fun anecdote.

Instead of saying you are a "really random person," tell them about your penchant for quoting bits of trivia whenever the mood strikes and your nervous habit of whistling the song "Stairway to Heaven." It's the same thing, but colorful.

When in doubt, go for humor. "Message me if you are changing the world or Paul Rudd" is one we'll gladly let you borrow.

DON'T REFERENCE PAST RELATIONSHIPS

"Just got out of a long-term relationship" doesn't just sound like you have some baggage, it sounds like you run the entire lost luggage department for Delta. It's good to be honest, but save the ex convo for later. If you don't want something serious, then just say what everyone else who just wants to bone says: "I'm just looking to have fun!" While we're on the topic, never write: "I'm new to this whole online dating thing . . . " This is similar to an *American Idol* (RIP) contestant prefacing their performance with, "I've had a cold all week." Nobody cares, just show us the goods.

CLEAN IT UP

Take time to clean up spelling errors and punctuation—your profile isn't a text message to your best friend. You aren't handwriting this thing! Spell-check is most likely alerting you with little red dotted lines that something has gone horribly wrong. If the OCD part of your brain doesn't motivate you to right-click and fix it, then maybe using the part of your brain that is tired of getting messages from dumb-dumbs will.

MORAL OF THE STORY

YOU NEVER GET A SECOND CHANCE AT A FIRST SWIPE

Your dating profile is your Internet handshake to a new stranger. Do you want a wimpy, half-assed grab or worse, a sweaty, lingering mess? Probably not. It takes as much time to wax your vageen as it does to wax poetic. Both are equally important aspects of dating. Oh, you're into the full bush thing so you didn't understand the previous comparison? No problem! It takes as much time to groom your bush as it does to write about your obsession with your favorite '90s band, Bush. Better? Great. The point is: Spend time on your profile.

Reading Between the Lines

Profile Says	This Means
"I like deep books that make me think about the meaning of it all. My favorite is *Catcher in the Rye*."	"I have not read a new book since my high school AP Lit class."
"The six things I could never do without are family, friends, food, water, good conversation, and my iPhone."	"I am a human being that was born on the planet Earth."
"I consider myself a male feminist."	"Sleep with me, smart girls."
"My mom says I'm funny!"	"I'm not funny."
"I'm looking for someone down-to-earth . . ."	". . . Because I am crazy uptight and that is the only kind of person who can deal with me."
(Blank Profile)	"My shirtless selfie posed next to this tiger should speak for itself."

WHO YOU ARE

TIWYS

You Leave No Mystery

The Witness and the Protection

You were living in a bad neighborhood years ago and witnessed some stuff you shouldn't have. You hoped to erase the memories and move on, but when the police needed a witness, like any good American citizen, you testified. Now, Manuel Madrigal from the EL-72 gang wants to have you off'ed.

Since the high-profile trial, you've begun your new life as Abigail O'Malley, thanks to the kind officers in the Witness Protection Program. Life in Overland Park, Kansas, isn't so bad. Kansas has good barbecue and your new cover as a yoga instructor has provided you with the namaste you needed after the stressful trial.

You were told that the U.S. Marshals Service has a 100% success rate in keeping witnesses who follow the program's guidelines alive and things were running smoothly . . . until you started dating again.

"You realize *we* set up your new cellphone," Officer Stanton tells you when he comes to meet you for your monthly checkup. "I can read all of your texts."

"So?"

"You texted a man named Ethan, 'Sorry I can't meet up. I have my Witness Protection Program officer coming over Friday night.'"

"Look, I thought it would be rude to write back and just say, 'No I can't meet up.' He probably thought I was joking anyway. What kind of person is even in the Witness Protection Program?"

"*You* are in the Witness Protection Program, Abigail!" he screams.

"Who's Abigail? . . . Oh, yeah. Me."

Stanton glares at you and loosens his tie.

"I need to sound exciting," you try to reason with him. "I swear, ever since I witnessed that quadruple homicide and testified before a grand jury my life has just gotten so boring. How am I supposed to make myself sound interesting to any cute new guys I meet?"

"There is a death warrant out for you, in case you forgot. This could be one of Madrigal's guys!" he says, pulling at his five o'clock shadow.

"Last week you posted a YouTube tutorial titled 'Before and After: See My 60-Day Witness Protection Makeover.' It's not a makeover. You changed your appearance so you won't get murdered. No social media. At all!"

"I used to be a 130-pound brunette and now I'm a 122-pound blond. I'm totally unrecognizable. That is called a makeover. What is the point of having this yoga body if I can't show it off?"

You pull up your shirt to show off your "yoga tummy" for proof.

"Madrigal has men all over the country looking for you!" he screams.

"Just to double-check, are all of these men definitely murderous savages? None of them could be misunderstood bad boys looking to meet, like, a really good listener? Just checking since, you know, they're looking for me anyway."

"They want to tie blocks of cement to your feet and drown you in the Hudson River. And you joined Twitter and tweeted,

'Day 37: Going to a Royals game tonight alone #100daysofsolitude' using the handle @MyNewNameIsAbby."

"First of all, my new name *is* Abby. Second of all, the guy I'm dating likes baseball and I want him to think I'm cool."

"You aren't even trying to follow the program guidelines! You also texted Ethan copies of your new driver's license."

"Look how good my blowout is in the photo!" you say, as you scramble through your purse to find your ID.

"This is really more of a safety issue," Stanton says, as he scribbles down notes about your wrongdoings in his pad. "But also, from a relationship standpoint with this Ethan guy, you are doing it all wrong."

This is when you realize Officer Stanton has never had to date in Overland Park.

"Excuse me?" you stammer. "I've had to move away from everything I've ever known. I've had to delete my Instagram account after years of artistic filtering. I've left my family, my friends, and Tinder prospects I spent days messaging back and forth before the trial. Do you even know how hard it is to maintain a conversation for that long with a guy on Tinder? Do you fucking know how many prospects there are in Overland Park's Tinder? Three! Fucking three matches! It is slim pickings out here and if there's a guy I like, I've got to lock that shit down!"

Within forty-eight hours, Stanton has relocated you to an empty cabin in the woods of Nebraska with no cell towers for miles, no Wi-Fi, and no gadgets.

Stanton hands you a sleeping bag and some firewood. "We'll drop off a package each Wednesday that will include enough food for the week, until we figure out how to seamlessly transition you into working with the woodsmen down the road. Do you have any survival questions?"

"Yes. Yes, I do. What *exactly* did you mean when you said I was 'doing it all wrong' from a 'relationship standpoint' with Ethan?"

"I'm leaving. We are done here."

"No! Wait. This *is* a survival question. Can I borrow your phone? I need to text Ethan a photo of my new digs and explain that I'm in lumberjack training in Nebraska. Would you be opposed to me dropping him a pin of where I am? Come back!"

Despite the efforts of the Witness Protection Program, the EL-72 gang discovers your whereabouts a few days later. However, Madrigal calls off the hit, telling his men that a life without Wi-Fi is a more sadistic torture than even he could imagine. ●

TOO MUCH TOO FAST

Everyone likes a chase. But it is impossible to chase something that is constantly charging toward you with information. If something comes too easy, it is human nature to think, "There must be something wrong with it" and become skeptical. Would you take a job if you didn't have to interview for it? No! That company is desperate. Would you take those free comedy tickets from those guys who harass you in Times Square? No! That comedy sucks. Would you join a sorority that doesn't make you rush? No! That sorority is for girls with sideburns. Life has taught us that you need to work for anything worthwhile.

MORAL OF THE STORY YOU SHOULD BE A RIDDLE, WRAPPED IN A MYSTERY, INSIDE AN ENIGMA

In a time when everyone feels the need to share everything with everyone, it can be hard to retrain your brain to hold some stuff back when you start dating a new guy. How will he know what a huge philanthropist you are unless you hit that handy-dandy little "Share" button after donating money to malnourished guinea pigs on CrowdRise? If you think you're lacking some mystery, here are some guidelines to getting it back:

DON'T OVEREXPLAIN

He asks you out but you can't make it (don't worry—you don't want to be too available anyway! See? You understand the chase!). But you strip any silver lining away from this rain cloud of conflicting plans when you then decide to give him a play-by-play of what you are doing instead. There is nothing wrong with a simple, "Oh no! I can't, I have plans. Would tomorrow work?" You're interested in him, but have other things going on. Perfect.

Where you go wrong is when you respond, "Oh no! I can't because I have happy hour drinks with my co-workers at 5 P.M., and then dinner with my roommate at 7 P.M., and then I'm going to my friend Ashley's birthday party. I feel like I haven't really been a good friend to her lately so I probably have to stay till the end and it won't be over until like 2 A.M."

Shut . . . up. Keep it simple! Maybe you're worried he'll think you're lying, not interested, or you want it documented where you'll be throughout the night in case you get abducted. Whatever the reason is, stop.

LET THE CONVO REST

You have interesting opinions on everything from how to solve the Israeli–Palestinian conflict to where the best tapas bar is in your city. Have conversations about that! Don't bore a guy you just started dating by Gchatting or texting him throughout the day when you don't really have anything to say. If you think that if he's talking to you he can't be talking to another girl, you're wrong. This is the one case where men are very good at multitasking.

Think about it, do you talk to your mom every day? Probably not *every* day and she won't stop calling you. See? It works! Leave him wanting more. Leave him feeling curious. Let him chase you. And take a nap.

DON'T TRY TO MAKE HIM JEALOUS

"I'll play it cool and won't text him. Instead, I will subtly live-blog my evening via Snapchat and Instagram. He'll see how much fun I'm having and text me first! Bonus points if I can snag a pic with a mystery man." If you are trying to make your sister jealous, this tactic might work for you. Your phone will be flooded with "Where the eff are you? Your life is insane!" texts and your mission will be complete.

But a guy responds to a little mystery. If he's wondering where you are, he's thinking about you and his interest is growing. So give him a chance to wonder!

MYSTERY MATCH!

Wait until a guy has earned your trust before you tell him all your secrets. See if you can match the appropriate wait time with the secret below!

Duration of Relationship	Your Secrets
First date	**A.** I talk to my dog in a British nanny voice.
Third date	**B.** I'd really like it if we could tickle each other's buttholes with feathers while listening to gentle orca whale sounds.
One month	**C.** I see dead people.
	D. I got arrested in high school for trying to steal a fanny pack from The Limited.
Three months	**E.** One time I hooked up with a guy who had two-and-a-half ballsacks. I Googled it and it's actually pretty common.
Six months	**F.** I accidentally killed our family's pet turtle when I was eight and blamed it on our dog.
One year	**G.** I have recurring nightmares about being chased up a down-moving escalator by Donald Duck while on my way to take a test.
Three years	**H.** My teeth are fake veneers. They got knocked out when a subway break dancer accidentally pop 'n locked me in the face.
Never	

Answer Key: First date: G. Third date: D. One month: E. Three months: H. Six months: B. One year: A. Three years: F. Never: C.

TIWYS

Your Imagination Runs Wild When He's MIA

The Brain and the Boy

On your first date with Alex, you leaned down to pet an adorable French bulldog and he (the dog) got an instant boner.

Now you and Alex have an inside joke and ever since, you two have been texting each other back and forth pictures of dogs and their disgusting little red rockets. Sure, it's only been a few months, but when he texted that his favorite show was *It's Always Sunny in Philadelphia* and you told him Dee and Mac are married in real life, you're pretty sure when he replied "awesome" he was referring specifically to marriage being "awesome" and was trying to bring up the conversation with you. So it was pretty cool of you to pretend you didn't notice and talk about the Philly bar scene instead. Basically you've achieved that delicate balance of interested but casual. Guys go crazy for that.

But one day, you text him and he doesn't write you back. You can't figure out why. Nobody goes from blowing up your phone to MIA the next day.

All of a sudden you feel it creeping in. The feeling. This has happened a few times before with other guys, but you thought it was a phase, or a thing of the past.

No. No. No. "Go away!" you tell the feeling.

The side effects of those happy crush endorphins have caused paranoia, delusions, and self-doubt. You know you are imagining things but are unable to stop yourself. The feeling tells you: Something must have happened to him.

"I think something happened," you tell your friend Julia, who, after much deliberation, you have decided to confide in before calling 911. "Maybe I should start calling local hospitals or check the Gowanus Canal for his body."

She gently tells you, "Sometimes you let your imagination run wild."

Julia doesn't understand at all. You try to explain. "Just yesterday he liked my #TGIF Instagram photo of an actual TGI Fridays restaurant."

"Well, it's not like he reGrammed you," she says bluntly. "Do you think maybe he just lost interest and made a confrontation-free getaway? Like an Irish exit, via text," she adds.

Ouch.

Not possible. Alex would never break your heart. You have an inside joke together, for fuck's sake. You picture yourself leading a search party for his dead body. You give the police dogs helping with the search the cardigan you wore on your first date because he hugged you and you're sure his scent is still on there.

Your friend is trying to talk sense into you, but you aren't listening. You stare into the distance and imagine what happened to him. "He was probably walking down the street in Midtown starting to text me back, but then . . . "

A robber approaches an old lady nearby and tries to grab her purse. Alex comes to the rescue! He uses tae kwon do moves and scares the robber off. Phew!

Julia is droning on, reminding you that it's only been a few hours since you last heard from him. "Maybe he's just busy!" she says.

You nod. "Maybe."

Alex is frazzled, but he's a red-blooded American hero and shakes it off. He picks up his phone to tell you all about his adventures when suddenly he encounters one of those street performers who dress up in silver face paint and do robot moves. Ain't nobody got time for that! Alex has places to go and people (you!) to text. He tries to sidestep the performer so he can text you. The next thing you know, they are pumping up the jam (to the song "Pump Up the Jam") in an epic dance battle. Alex pops and locks his way into glory. Angered by his public defeat, the robot performer spins Alex into an open pothole. Ahhhhh!

"Maybe his phone is in the other room and he hasn't seen your text," Julia continues. Again, you appease her. "Could be."

Alex must return to his beloved, so he crawls his way to freedom using an axe he carved out of a rock with an even sharper rock. Victory! He is promptly hit by a cab. Broken and bloodied, he uses his only still-functioning body part, his pointer finger, in an attempt to text you back. Out of nowhere a majestic American bald eagle swoops in and clutches his phone in its claws, flying off into the horizon.

"You know it is like extremely rare to see a bald eagle in the middle of a busy metropolis, right?" Julia sneers.

Whoops. Did you say all of that out loud? Time to confess.

"That scenario is literally the only thing that makes sense," you insist.

Or is it? . . . ●

WHAT HAPPENS NEXT

Very much like the game *Clue*, there are several possible endings when you don't immediately hear back from a guy.

SCENARIO 1: HE DOES "THE FADE AWAY"

Also known as ghosting, a disappearing act, an Irish exit, peacing out, silent but deadly, the runaway, invisible inking, icing, melting, evaporating, "I was never here," The Phantom Menace, The Phantom of the Opera, the David Blaine, the David Copperfield, the David Bernstein (That's our dentist. He does magic too), the smoke and mirrors, the smoke machine, the Alzheimer's, the Casper, the Fade Dunaway, and the black hole.

We know your date went incredibly well. We know he talked about things you two would do in the future. But fading away was so much easier than having to talk to you and explain that for whatever reason he wasn't into it anymore. This has nothing to do with you. Nothing you do will change his mind. You will never hear from him again.

What to do: Pretend he never existed. And for god's sake, do not text him.

Alex

Hey check out this photo of a puppy boner

Your first inside joke!

Haha it's so tiny! He looks embarrassed

Answering texts at two-minute intervals. Again, he is totally into you.

Not as embarrassed as when u fell off the stage at your 1st ballet recital ;)

He paid attention to stories you told and he is referencing that now, thus indicating interest!

So true! How's work?

Pretty busy. So, happy hour this Friday?

Perf...where should we go?

Hey there workaholic! Looking forward to drinks ;)

So srsly where should we go <u>tonight</u>?

Are you dead?

Just saw a dog boner outside! So funny, right?

YOU ARE AN UNFORGIVABLE MONSTER

SCENARIO 2: YOU HEAR FROM HIM A WEEK LATER

Just when you think a guy has done "the fade away," he will call you up like it's no big thing. This is the same guy who will cancel your date an hour before because his friend had an extra Knicks ticket. This is the same guy who will ask you out on a Monday for a Friday night date, you won't hear from him all week, and then Friday at 9 P.M. he asks you to meet him and his friends for drinks in an hour. This is same guy who sends nonchalant sweet and flirty texts, but then ignores simple questions like, "Leaving my house now, what's the address we're meeting at?" He confuses you. He plays with your heart. This guy is worse than the fade away because he will lead you on forever and before you even realize it, you have become his go-to booty call.

What to do: Like heroin, just say no.

SCENARIO 3: HE BREAKS IT OFF

If he's a stand-up guy, he'll be man enough to be open and honest about his feelings. Maybe he broke up with his girlfriend, started dating around a bit, but decided to get back together with her. He wanted to let you know because he hopes you two can still be friends. You won't be friends, but you should still appreciate his honesty.

What to do: While your ego is bruised, before you scream, "Glad I was so awful that I made you run back into the arms of your ex-girlfriend! Asshole!" or, "I didn't even like you anyway! Asshole!" or, just "Asshole!" remember, he respected you so much as a woman that he chose the road less traveled, the gentle letdown.

SCENARIO 4: HE TEXTS YOU

Two hours later, you get a text along with a picture of a puppy boner. He was working and is so sorry for the delay. You don't initially hear your phone buzz over the sound of your own sobs or Adele's "Someone Like You." When you finally pick up your phone, your anxiety slowly subsides and you can't even remember what sent you into that downward spiral.

What to do: You don't text him back immediately because, you know, you don't want to come off as crazy. You're a chill chick.

SCENARIO 5: EVERYTHING IN YOUR HEAD WAS TRUE

The bald eagle. The dance-off. The robbery. The near-death hit-and-run. It was all true. It's happened. We once heard a friend of a friend of a friend dated a guy who went missing for six months after their first date, only to contact her when he woke up from a coma. They're engaged now. But before you cling to this possibility as a beacon of hope, you should know this is incredibly rare.

What to do: In the case your predictions turn out to be true, give TLC a call. They're looking for a show to run after *Long Island Medium*.

MORAL OF THE STORY
YOUR FICTION IS STRANGER THAN THE TRUTH

As frustrating as it is, there isn't much you can do to control how a guy responds, when he responds, or whether he responds at all. No matter how many times you've read *The Secret*, you cannot *will* the text to come. But what you can control is the level of stress this causes you. It isn't productive imagining all of the worst possible scenarios (He found another girl! He joined a Buddhist monk monastery and took a vow of silence! The NSA must be intercepting my texts after I texted my friend "You're da bomb.com," which accidentally sent her a link on how to build bombs.). So before you go through all five stages of grief in the fifteen minutes since you last talked to a guy, just remember: If a guy isn't getting back to you within a reasonable amount of time, he's not worth your time—or your imagination—anyways.

TIWYS

No One Is Forever 21

The Old Woman and the Flower Crown

You've got a hot date coming up with a new guy and the outfits in your closet aren't doing it for you. You make a run to your go-to store for cheap, sexy, and disposable fashion: Forever 21. You begin browsing the racks, sifting through skirts made of vegan leather (the material formerly known as pleather) and a knock-off of a knock-off of a knock-off of H&M's latest knock-off of a Marc Jacobs black fishnet dress.

A salesman named Rufus, in a too-tight black shirt and side bangs, approaches you.

"Hey there, sweet thing! Anything special you're looking for?" Rufus asks.

You look up, holding a metallic gold crop top.

"I'm looking for something fun and flirty," you say. "I'm going out with a new guy."

His ears perk up with excitement.

"A hot date!" he squeals. "So fab! And what a fierce top you're holding. You can wear anything you want . . . when you're twenty-one."

Oh my god, don't you love Rufus? He has no idea your college ID is decaying at the bottom of your purse somewhere and you recently bought your first pair of Spanx.

"You are so sweet!" you tell him. "I mean, I wish."

"You are twenty-one, aren't you?" he hisses.

You're a little taken aback. What is it with him and the age thing? You can take a compliment but sheesh! You smile and keep shopping.

"How fucking old are you?"

Suddenly Rufus's tone is less Tim Gunn and more, "Freeze! I've got a gun."

"Jesus, no, I'm not twenty-one," you say.

"You can't shop at Forever 21 if you're over twenty-one. Leave the store now ... Oh, you're not leaving? You're not gonna leave? Fine!"

Rufus grabs his walkie-talkie and jumps into emergency mode. "Security! I need backup! We have a Code Old Person. I repeat. Code Old Person."

Before you can ask what the hell is going on, a butch security man named Diesel appears.

"Is this another over-age situation? I'm gonna need to see your ID," demands Diesel. "Ew, says you were born before 1997. Gross. And you really thought you could shop here?"

You point out how the sign on the store says *Forever* 21.

"Duh, *the clothes* stay forever twenty-one. You just get old," explains Diesel. "What do you think this place is, L.L. Bean?"

They cackle. "Good one, Diez!" says Rufus.

He shifts his attention and notices the hurt in your eyes, as well as the beginning stages of crow's feet.

"Look, you seem sweet," says Rufus. "It has nothing to do with you. This is coming from corporate. We can't have all these old biddies wearing our clothes for twenty-one-year-olds. It hurts the brand. We're gonna need you to leave the premises immediately."

You tell Rufus and Diesel how you shop at Forever 21 all of the time, how you love their cheap clothes, and it's all you can afford with your shit post-entry-level job that still pays an entry-level job salary despite two promotions, and how you come here all the time to buy mass-produced flower crowns and strategically faded faux vintage shirts.

"Don't do this!" you protest. "Look, you even have a *Third Rock from the Sun* shirt. I grew up watching this show. This shirt is made for me!"

As you grab at the extra-small tee, you notice a neon sign that reads "November—Remember the '90s Month."

You start to cry.

A young teen walks in and spots the shirt you are holding and snatches it from your palms.

"Oh my goddd there are old people on that shirt. It's like so old. I bet everyone on that shirt is dead now. It's like a really, old, gross shirt and I love it. Vintage. I want it. Gimme."

Teenie runs to the register clasping the tee. Those perky breasts. That fresh baby skin. You can't compete with that!

"We need you to leave, ma'am," says Diesel.

"Ma'am? I am not a *ma'am*!" you wail.

That is the last straw. You start grabbing clothes off the racks, trying to fit them over your head. You have handfuls of clothes— lace, sequined, and fringed. You're tossing clothing racks aside. People are recording your tantrum on their iPhones.

"I just want to look hot for my date!" you scream. "I can't have my dating profile picture be me in a sensible suit from Ann Taylor!"

The clothes aren't fitting over your head and Diesel and Rufus have started to call for more backup as they wrestle you to the ground. "We need you to put the clothes down immediately!" they warn.

It's no use. You are completely possessed.

"Your sizes are fucked up here!" you scream as they carry you out of the store.

You will never return. You have learned the hard truth: No one stays forever twenty-one. ●

	Babies "R" Us	Old Navy	Abercrombie & Fitch
Suggested Age	Fetus to 3 years old	4 to 13 years old	14 to 15 years old (think of it like cocaine: everyone should try it once but then quickly realize it's not a good look)
Ideal Customer	Babies are them!	Generic kids who have no say in anything	Teenage douchebags
Biggest Competitor	Grandma and her knitting needles	Your sibling's hand-me-downs	Hot Topic (if they don't go douche, they go goth)
Most Popular Purchase	Birth control (you buy it after you leave the store)	American flag anything	Nothing. You just come to look at the shirtless male models who stand at the door
Pet Peeve	Uncovered electrical outlets	When your head seamstress calls in from Bangladesh and asks if she can have the night off for her preschool graduation	Ugly people
Best Known For	Being the Costco of babies	Performance fleece, oh it's fine!	A scent that won't leave your body for days after you exit the store

	Urban Outfitters	J.Crew	Kohl's
Suggested Age	16 to 24 years old	25 to 39 years old	40 years old to death
Ideal Customer	Young people trying to look unique by shopping at a chain store, like everyone else	Waspy hipsters with jobs	Someone who serves on the PTA or has a good pot roast recipe
Biggest Competitor	Your kitchen scissors and a DIY tie-dye kit	Flea market costume jewelry	Anywhere with a coupon
Most Popular Purchase	Rompers and other things you haven't worn since you were an eight-year-old on Easter Sunday	Whatever it is, it buttons all the way up to the top	Pantsuits designed by Lauren Conrad
Pet Peeve	Jeans that naturally get knee holes	People who don't get how to layer	Crying kids who want to leave before you're ready
Best Known For	Dressing every person who attends Coachella	Business on top, sequined miniskirt on the bottom	Your one-stop shop for shower curtains, items "Seen On TV!," and where dreams go to die

PULLING OFF YOUR LOOK

We wish people didn't judge a book by its cover, but a cover is also how you tell the difference between *War and Peace* and a *My Little Pony* coloring book. While it's bad enough that those around you will make insta-judgments based on how you're dressing, you'll be doing yourself a disservice if you're trying to pull off a look that just isn't you.

Doing this will only make you look like you're having a quarter-life crisis or a one-third-life crisis (applicable to ladies in their thirties with healthy older relatives or ladies in their twenties with a family history of dying young). Look, if you've got it, flaunt it. But the type of guys you attract by dressing like a ho-bag are probably not nice, future-worthy men anyway. If the only difference between your slutty witch Halloween costume and your work clothes is a pointy hat, you might need to rethink your wardrobe.

MORAL OF THE STORY 21-YEAR-OLD FEATHERS DO NOT MAKE 21-YEAR-OLD BIRDS

Try these tips for finding clothes that showcase you in the best way:

- Learn what is flattering on *you* (no matter how skinny you are, everyone gets those mini vaginas in their armpits when you wear something strapless).
- Learn how to attract the type of men *you* are looking for (if that's men at auto shows, then booty shorts and bikini tops all the way).
- Figure out who *you* are at the earliest age possible (take a cue from little lady Shiloh Jolie-Pitt, who has owned the casual menswear look since birth).
- Still at a loss? Change your Tinder preference to "women" so you can use the app to get outfit ideas from real females. Left-swipe your way through the many boob-heavy mirror selfies and you'll actually find some color combination ideas for spring!

Remember this information the next time you go to the mall looking for that hot date-night outfit and see a pair of checkered purple hot pants in the window. You're not sure about them, but you start to think that maybe if you pair them with a beanie and some wool socks they'll be a little more subtle and you can totally pull them off. Maybe. Maybe not. The important thing is, you do you.

You Have FOMO

The Intervention and the Party Girl

You're on your way home from work, scrolling through various feeds and event calendars of no less than seventeen different websites and blogs for tips on what the hottest events of the night are. You open the door to your apartment and find a gathering of your six closest loved ones seated in a semicircle in your living room.

You giddily clap your hands.

"This is some kind of early birthday surprise, isn't it? You guys are the best!"

"I think you should sit down," says your friend Emma, her voice somber, her eyes staring at the ground. "This is an intervention."

Oh, crap. You *did* overdo it with the tequila shots the other night and tap her boyfriend's wiener.

"I'm really sorry I touched Morgan's dick," you apologize. "I think of him like a brother. I mean, not that I touch my brother's dick, but it was a platonic dick grab. Look, it won't happen again."

Emma remains calm. She explains that she doesn't care about the sexual harassment or your drinking problem. The reason for this intervention is more serious than alcoholism.

"You are suffering from FOMO," she states.

All you can do to respond is a simple, "FOMO?"

"Fear of Missing Out. It's gotten out of control," chimes your cousin Molly. "We're here for you."

"Whoa," you say. "You guys. You're being a little irrational. I'm a young, social girl. I like to go out and have fun. I can stop any time I want. I'm not addicted."

You check yourself into Foursquare for your intervention and tag everyone in the room.

"You made us leave our family camping trip one hour in because there was no cell reception to Insta-brag about how much fun you were having," says Molly.

You avoid eye contact, but mumble under your breath, "If a tree falls in a forest and I don't Instagram it, did it even happen?"

Your co-worker Penelope confronts you. "You flew to Dallas last Thursday and showed up at the Hilton after I Instagrammed a picture from my bat mitzvah. It was Throwback Thursday! That party happened over a decade ago."

This one was your bad. Sure, you should have thought a little more logically about the situation when you saw the scrunchies and crunchy bangs featured in the "Hava Nagila" photo, but you read a trend piece in the *New York Times* about how having bar and bat mitzvahs later in life is all the rage. You wanted to show your support! And, if you're being honest, you wanted to meet a nice Jewish boy.

Your roommate, Lucy, who has been somberly weeping, speaks up.

"You showed up to every Facebook event in the city yesterday: a dog fashion show, a naked Hula-Hoop contest, a middle-school graduation party, a crème brûlée–eating contest, an abstract sound poetry reading, a Third Eye Blind cover band concert, a Walt Whitman flash mob, a women's suffrage reenactment, and the screening of a documentary about Scotch tape. You were blowing up my newsfeed. We're worried about you. We think you need to go away for some time, disconnect, go off the grid."

Lucy grabs the phone out of your palm.

Your friends don't understand what missing out can lead to. You don't know which event the love of your life might be at. You don't know which event will be *the* event all your friends talk about for the next year. So you go to them all.

You snatch your phone back, grab your purse, and storm out of your apartment. You unlock your phone and begin scrolling through the night's event options again. If being at the coolest parties and events all of the time is a disease, then you must have a disease.

Wait a second.

"Oh my god," you stammer. "Do I really have FOMO?" ●

THE ROAD TO RECOVERY

Admitting you have FOMO is the first step toward recovery. A dependency problem with FOMO can have devastating effects not only on yourself, but also on those around you. It is typical that someone suffering from FOMO is unaware of these effects, as she is too distracted thinking of a witty caption for her most recent status update.

A FOMO addict is always distracted, responding to multiple group texts with her ladies on the ground trying to find out the best party to go to. Typical questions include: "Are there hot guys?" "Is it an open bar?" "How long is the line?" "On a scale of Aubrey's Friday night Yahtzee 'party' to that disco-foam rager in 2012, how would you rate where you are?" If you're at every gathering all of the time, a night out loses its enchantment. There will always be new inside jokes to be made, and parties to attend, and your friends are not going to replace you if you skip a night out every once in a while.

MORAL OF THE STORY
THE ONLY THING WE HAVE TO FEAR IS "FEAR OF MISSING OUT" ITSELF

While a FOMO addict joneses to see and be seen, she ironically misses the opportunity to form real connections with the people around her. Besides, comparing your life to other people's action-packed Instagram feeds will only drive you crazy.

Why stay in the moment instead of capture it? Well, like Ferris Bueller said, "Life moves pretty fast. If you don't stop and look around once in a while, you could miss it." (Good life tip: John Hughes movie quotes usually hold the answers to all of life's important questions.)

People with FOMO are simply no fun in more casual, low-key settings, which is the only time you can truly get to know someone you're interested in and build a relationship. Relationships fizzle and die when a quiet, intimate date night at home is disrupted by a craving for another hit. No, not another hit of crack cocaine, another hit of the Like button for the series of photos you could post from that new gallery opening or dance party with the DJ of the moment.

Learn to live a balanced life by staying home "one day at a time." Stay away from that "first party." If there is no first one, there cannot be a tenth one.

DO YOU SUFFER FROM FOMO?

*Twelve Questions Only **You** Can Answer*

1. Have you ever decided to stop going out for a week or so, but only lasted a couple of days? **Yes / No**

2. Do you wish people would mind their own business about your partying and stop telling you what to do? **Yes / No**

3. Have you ever switched from one kind of event (a house party!) to another (a themed house party!) in the hope that this would make you bored and want to go home? **Yes / No**

4. Have you had to look at your calendar immediately upon awakening during the past year? **Yes / No**

5. Do you envy people who go to better parties than you? **Yes / No**

6. Have you had conflicts connected with overscheduling your calendar during the past year? **Yes / No**

7. Has your party hopping caused trouble at home? **Yes / No**

8. Do you ever try to "skip to the front of the line" because you don't want to wait? **Yes / No**

9. Do you tell yourself you can go home any time you want to, even though you keep checking Instagram to see if there's anything better happening? **Yes / No**

10. Have you missed days of work or school for a sample sale?
Yes / No

11. Do you use a "black-and-white" photo filter? **Yes / No**

12. Have you ever felt that your life would be better if you were home sleeping? **Yes / No**

Results: Did you answer YES four or more times? If so, you are probably in trouble with FOMO. If you suffer from FOMO, follow our twelve-step recovery program with FOMO Anonymous (FOMOA). FOMOA (rhymes with the Girl Scout cookie) is a fellowship of men and women who share their experience, strength, and hope. The only requirement for membership is a desire to stop FOMO . . . and confirmation that your name is on our VIP list. Just kidding. Those VIP days are behind you now.

WARNING: It is possible to develop FOMO about cooler, better FOMO Anonymous meetings with hotter, funner people also suffering from FOMO.

THE TWELVE STEPS: A FOMO RECOVERY PROGRAM

1. We admitted we were powerless over our calendar—that our lives had become unmanageable.

2. Came to believe that a Power greater than ourselves (Snapchat) could destroy our sanity.

3. Made a decision to turn our will and our iPhone over to the care of our BFF, as we understood Him or Her.

4. Made a searching and fearless wardrobe inventory of our party clothes.

5. Admitted to ourselves, to another human being, and in a six-second looping Vine post, the exact nature of our wrongs.

6. Were entirely ready to have a BFF remove all these defects of character, via deleting a lot of embarrassing photos.

7. Humbly asked BFF to also remove our drunk Tweets.

8. Made a list of all persons we had harmed in bar fights, club promoters we had offended, and bartenders we undertipped, and became willing to make amends to them all.

9. Made direct amends to such people wherever possible (although it may be difficult to track them down due to their own FOMO), except when to do so would injure them or others.

10. Continued to take personal inventory and when we were wrong promptly admitted it in a TMI Tumblr post.

11. Sought through prayer and meditation to improve our conscious contact with our BFF, as we understood Him or Her, praying only for knowledge of BFF's will for us and the power to stay home and watch a *Friends* marathon on Netflix together.

12. Having had a spiritual awakening (thanks to wheatgrass shots over body shots) as the result of these Steps, we tried to carry this message to others suffering from FOMO, and to practice these principles in all our affairs.

You Don't Know When to Sleep with Him

The Revolutionary and the Uprising

You follow the directions you received earlier that day and arrive at a charming macaron shop on a quiet street. You look cautiously side-to-side before delivering the secret password to the tattooed girl delicately arranging a colorful macaron tower behind the counter.

"Do you have any *chocolat citron vert* macarons?" you inquire with an arched eyebrow.

"Ah, yes," she replies, abandoning her tower. "We keep all the macarons with *chocolat* in the back. Let me show you."

You follow her through a door behind the pastel pink refrigerator and crawl through a narrow passageway into a dimly lit secret back room. You push your way through a crowd that's at least a hundred deep and discover a meeting already in full swing of like-minded young rebels in the midst of planning a revolution.

"Sisters! Comrades! Gather round," the woman standing on a stool in the center of the room calls out. You've never seen her before but you immediately recognize who she is from the descriptions in the underground press materials that led to your interest in this cause. Jacqueline Delacroix. She's a petite woman wearing a crimson beret over a sleek black bob and is surrounded by the thick white smoke of her cigarette.

"The time for action is now. How long have we suffered at the hands of the current regime? They who have decreed the fourth date as . . . the 'sex date.'"

The crowd murmurs in agreement as you squirm through the throng to get closer.

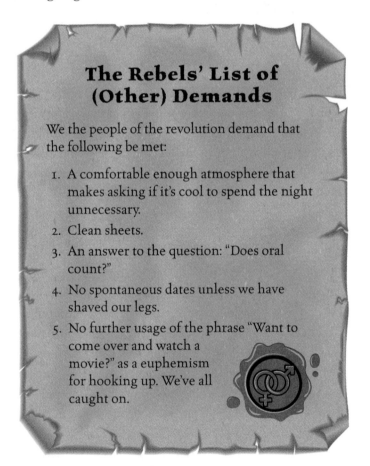

The Rebels' List of (Other) Demands

We the people of the revolution demand that the following be met:

1. A comfortable enough atmosphere that makes asking if it's cool to spend the night unnecessary.
2. Clean sheets.
3. An answer to the question: "Does oral count?"
4. No spontaneous dates unless we have shaved our legs.
5. No further usage of the phrase "Want to come over and watch a movie?" as a euphemism for hooking up. We've all caught on.

"This is a decision that should be left to the people! Not made by some coterie of opportunists. We, the single, are miserable. *Les misérables*, in fact. The nation is being fed lies by women's magazines and pop culture. It is left to us to reverse the establishment and claim the 'sex date' to be any date we so choose!"

"*Vive la résistance!*" a wide-eyed young insurgent cries out. "I grapple with this rule of law every time I meet a new man. Sometimes I want to have sex after two dates, sometimes after ten. I fear being labeled either a slut or a prude. We must regain control. A *coup d'état* is in order!"

Jacqueline applauds the young woman's enthusiasm. "I dream a dream of five dates gone by, with no sexual pressure. Our community has been ravaged by an outbreak of the belief that their status as 'girlfriend material' lies in the balance of when they are prepared to make love with a new partner."

Jacqueline goes on. "*Mes amis*, we have attempted nonviolent, civil resistance. We have written think pieces for *Jezebel*, held all-night vigils outside the apartment of Candace Bushnell. And still there are no answers, no change. Only confusion about what the right number of dates is."

"This law is the Anne Hathaway of laws!" a woman yells. "It's actually not the worst law but it's the law I hate the most."

"What if I want to use handcuffs on the third date? How do I know if that is okay?" someone else cries out. "Will I be judged or praised?"

"Let us not forget our predecessors, those women who lost their lives during the great BDSM Revolution of 1999. In their name, we should use handcuffs at any time we so choose."

A street urchin appears, waving a giant red flag, and the members of the uprising flood out of the macaron shop and onto the streets. The women build a dusty barricade, comprised of a CB2 tweed ottoman, a plastic storage bin from Target, and an IKEA closet that rises high into the sky.

As the rain begins to fall, a young girl in tattered clothes sings, *"On my own, pretending he's inside me."*

You cock your head to the side. "I don't think I know that song."

"I'm only on date number three with this new guy I'm seeing and I'm just so horny. But we'll be together . . . in one date more."

The girl's phone vibrates. She unlocks the screen and abruptly collapses to the ground upon reading the text.

"Oh, no! You're injured!" you cry, rushing toward her.

"Do not fret," she whispers, trembling, shot down by the words in the text message. "He is cancelling our plans for this evening. What if I never see him again? As long as the current laws are in place, I'll have to wait another four dates to have sex. If only . . . " She trails off.

"If only what?" you beg.

"If only . . . I had sex . . . sooner . . . like I wanted to."

She takes a final breath and slumps into your arms. Jacqueline appears. She lowers her head and places a hand on your shoulder.

"She is the first of us to fall upon this barricade," she says quietly, her volume slowly increasing with rage. "We fight here in her name. She will not die in vain!" ●

THE DECISION

We're told it's all about timing—the exact moment you decide to show him your vagina could be the difference between a one-night stand and a lifetime commitment. This pressure can lead to a lot of post-coital guilt and pre-coital blue lady-balls.

It also leads to a lot of strange rationalizing. Girls find themselves saying things like: "I'll come home with you, but *nothing is going to happen.*" Your brain splits off in a million different directions, as if this were sexual arithmetic (rate by which he answers text messages – the number of minutes he was late × how many dinners he paid for + flowers received + number of dates). You fail to live in the moment, which would allow you to use your instinct about what the right choice is.

MORAL OF THE STORY ABSTAIN AND ENJOY. SCREW AND ENJOY. REALLY, WHATEVER YOU'RE COMFORTABLE WITH

Do you know how many times a guy has heard a girl say, "I swear I *never* do this"? Maybe you really have *never* done this, but if you are doing "this" now, it really doesn't matter whether it's the first time or the tenth in the guy's eyes. Want to know what doesn't sound "skanky"? Just owning it! If you feel a connection, or you just really want to have sex, then have sex. Make it your decision, and don't preface it with this weird guilt dance. It makes the guy feel weird and it makes you look like someone who lacks confidence in her decisions, which isn't attractive to anyone.

If you're genuinely feeling guilty about having sex too soon, you probably aren't actually ready and you should wait. There is no shame in that. In fact, here is a bit of trivia for you: If you lose your virginity late in life, you will develop amazing blow job skills, much like how blind people naturally develop great hearing!

Cuddle Positions That Will Drive Your Man *CRAZY*

Not ready to do the deed but feeling a little cuddle horny? Try these kinky moves to get all of the friction without the penetration!

Little Spoon

It's the missionary of cuddle positions. But just like missionary, there's a reason it's a classic! If you want to take a new spin on a beloved favorite, try also sweetly holding his hand and turning on a movie. Pull that trick a couple times and he'll be calling you T-Spoon for T-rrific in bed! WARNING: Beware of something poking you in the lower back.

Big Spoon

Do you like the taste of back hair? Want to put those extra-long arms to use? Then this is the move for you. Surprise him one night by getting behind him and squeezing real tight. Guys love a girl that takes care of her own pleasure. When you're in control, you decide how fast or slow you fall asleep. He'll especially appreciate this one if he suffers from "tiny T-Rex arms" or "limp noodle arms." For extra pleasure, use a pillow to support your head.

Facing Each Other

This move is only for those more advanced and adventurous cuddlers. When done incorrectly, you both may have difficulty breathing, because you are mere inches from each other's face sharing the same air supply. However, master the proper head tilt and you can last all night long in this position. If he goes limp give his biceps a quick tickle. He'll be back to full hugging power in no time.

Texting While He Rubs Your Back

This one hits a real sweet spot for the ladies! In the last forty-five-minutes since you started banging, you've missed out on tons of texts from your friends. If you want to catch up on world events and weekend plans, try this complex move. He'll be so excited by the opportunity to pleasure his woman, he'll forget all about any reciprocation (later on when he's checking his fantasy football stats and you're too tired to give him a back scratch).

Sleeping While He Stares at You Adoringly

If you and your man have no shame satisfying your own needs, you will both love this one! Pass out in any position that feels comfortable. Don't worry about having a pretty resting face. Just like your O face, you're not supposed to look good if you're doing it right. He can curl up in his own tiny ball, while you each drift off into one pleasurable unconscious dream state. Hot!

cuddling \ kədl \ *v* **1 :** The act of tenderly embracing a romantic interest in a hug-like position with no direct genital stimulation. Spooning (where two bodies fit against each other in a spoon-like shape) is the predominant cuddle position. Cuddling may also be referred to as snuggling, nuzzling, nestling, petting, canoodling, hugging, holding, caressing, embracing, smooshing, mooshing, squeezing, and other things you do to adorable kittens.

TIWYS

You're Selling Yourself Short

The Infomercial and the Dreamer

You lay in bed solo as Saturday night turns into Sunday morning, watching a convincing infomercial salesman hawk dog swimmies. You don't own a dog, but think maybe you need these anyway? If only you could sell yourself that well.

Earlier that evening, you stumbled through an extremely awkward first date where you referred to your apartment's decor as "nursing home chic" and your curly hair as "poodle tongue meets light socket." You sigh and slowly drift off into dreamland as Ace, the dog swimmie pitchman, drones on . . . Zzzz . . .

Dream Pitch

Ace: Hey, it's your guy Ace here with my girl ShelbWow! "What exactly *is* ShelbWow," you ask? Why, it's Shelby Weinstein, a twenty-five-year-old freelancer, amateur botanist, and dedicated writer looking for love! She's got the soothing nature of your mother, the adventurous spirit of your best friend (she's always down for a last-minute beach excursion to Mexico!), and the spunk of your beautiful, overachieving childhood crush, *Saved By the Bell*'s Jessie Spano. This little wonder is very versatile. With her flexible, durable nature, you can take her anywhere—a book reading, hot yoga, a smelly RV en route to Burning Man— and she is always gonna be comfortable and happy! No more pouty faces, no more impossible-to-open-up emotional barriers. The first thirty days you spend with her are gonna completely change your life. This is why we'll give you our money-back guarantee. That's any money you spend on her during the first month you know one another, returned to you if you're not 100% thrilled with your investment. That's how much we believe in the power of ShelbWow! But wait, there's more! ShelbWow is a real self-starter and paid her own way through college. You'd be out of your mind not to jump on this opportunity! ShelbWow was created in Omaha, Nebraska, so you know she's a winner. That's also the birthplace of other game-changers like Warren Buffett, Malcolm X, and the bobby pin! Don't take my word for it, ask her roommate! They're really close.

Roommate: I just couldn't live without her!

Ace: Now you can have it all with ShelbWow! Simply call 1-800-WOW-SHEL. Call within the next twenty minutes and we will throw in a free back rub, normally valued at three dinner dates!

You grumble and turn over in your bed, only half awake. That was a good dream. Shelby seems nice . . . Zzzz . . .

Nightmare Pitch

Ace: Uh, hi. Excuse me? Sorry to bother you. I won't take up too much of your time. Have you met Shelby Weinstein? She's a twenty-five-year-old, unemployed, occasional pot-smoker and dedicated Tweeter looking for love. She babies you like your mother, is as irresponsible as your best friend (she ended up in a Mexican prison in Tijuana), and dealt with an addiction to over-the-counter caffeine pills like your childhood crush, *Saved By the Bell*'s Jessie Spano. This little wonder is very manic. With her irritable, fragile nature, you can take her anywhere—a book reading, hot yoga, a smelly RV en route to Burning Man— and she is always gonna find something to complain about. She'll be a complete misery! The first thirty days you spend with her are gonna complicate your life. This is why we've developed a very simple, money-back guarantee on any returns. That's any money you spend on her during the first month you know one another, returned to you when you are inevitably 100% under- whelmed with your investment. That's how much we believe in a flexible return policy. But wait, there's something you should know! Shelby went to a very cheap online college that is being investigated by the U.S. Department of Education. You'd be well advised to put in some serious thought before jumping on this opportunity. Shelby was created in Omaha, Nebraska, so it's a miracle that she's as normal as she is. That's also the birthplace of such questionable characters as Nick Nolte, Katie Holmes's ex-fiancé Chris Klein, and the man who invented those unhealthy TV dinners. Don't take my word for it, ask her room- mate. They're really close.

Roommate: Can you please tell her to stop stealing my clothes?

Ace: We'll give you a free trial, what do you have to lose? Just call 1-800-WOW-SHEL. Call within the next twenty minutes and we will throw in some free bed sheets. You will need them when she gets wasted.

You wake up in a cold sweat and shut off your TV. What happened to nice Shelby? You realize two things:

1. You really need to work on how you talk about yourself before you start to sound like a nightmare.

2. You cannot live without those damn dog swimmies. ●

WHAT'S MISSING? YOUR CONFIDENCE

Ever heard someone say: "Yeah, my job sounds cooler than it actually is" or "Sure, I do a lot of charity work, but doesn't everybody?" or "Sure, I look skinny now, but without these control-top leggings I'm a real heifer"?

Even the most wonderful people, those who bring so much to the table, can lack confidence. When prompted to speak about themselves—which is a common occurrence on a first date—they discredit or deny any positive attributes. Do you think that Ruth Bader Ginsburg got to where she is by telling people, "It really isn't that big a deal to be an Associate Justice of the Supreme Court. I mostly just sit around in this dumb-looking robe with a doily around my neck"? Probably not. That liberal trailblazing badass bitch has confidence.

MORAL OF THE STORY

PEOPLE WILL DATE YOU IF YOU WOULD DATE YOURSELF

You need to learn how to sell yourself. Remember the fairy tale, "*The Emperor's New Clothes*"? Those salespeople were so convincing about their product (which, if you remember, *did not actually exist*) that they persuaded a grown man to walk around town balls-ass-naked. If those jokers can passionately sell someone invisible pants, you can surely take the real, multidimensional, and unique things about you and make a case for them. So don't be afraid to mention your impressive degree, your half-marathon time, or the weekly volunteer work you do reading to underprivileged children the next time you're on a date. If you talk about yourself in a confident way, guys will see you as what you are—a great catch.

And remember, how you feel about yourself can't be determined by other people—so focus on building your own self-worth outside of a relationship. A happy relationship is like a board game expansion pack—it's only good if the original game is already amazing. Settlers of Catan is brilliant all on its own, but purchase the "Traders & Barbarians" add-on? Suddenly, creating settlements across a mystical island becomes all the more colorful. And rugged! You need to be able to look at yourself solo and see a fully completed masterpiece that you are proud of before you start thinking about an addition.

Lessons in Salesmanship

The exact same item can be made to sound life-changingly wonderful or heart-stoppingly awful. It's all about how you see it.

Product	Official Slogan	Rejected Slogan
Snuggie	"The blanket with sleeves!"	"One knot away from a straitjacket!"
Proactiv	"Get the clear skin you deserve!"	"Act fast before your high school years traumatize you for life."
Thighmaster	"Just put it between your knees and squeeze!"	"Just put it into your closet and never use it again!"
Slap Chop	"You'll be in a great mood all day 'cause you'll be slapping your troubles away!"	"You may be in a great mood all day, but it probably has nothing to do with finely chopping your vegetables."
Shake Weight	"Dump the dumbbell!"	"The most sexual thing to do at the gym since the glute bridge or squats."
George Foreman Grill	"Knock out the fat!"	"You're too lazy to use a real grill because you are fat."

YOUR
TYPE

147

You May Be Dating a Man Child

The Diner and the Dater

You sit nervously squirming in one of those fancy Italian restaurants with a name you can't pronounce that your blind date has picked out. The only thing you recognize on the menu is "quail eggs" and those tend to look like something a Smurf would eat for dinner or make their home in. So, no thank you. You look down at your chipped aqua-blue nail polish, remember you probably left your curling iron plugged in, and think: "I am not grown up enough for this situation."

Carter, dressed in a smart, single-breasted charcoal suit, saunters your way. His skin glows, his light brown hair is parted perfectly on the left, and he towers over other patrons at the restaurant. You've sent a couple texts back and forth, and have seen photos of him that your mutual friend showed you, but holy crap. He's so much more than you were expecting and you haven't even said a word to him yet. He knows everyone at the restaurant and does one of those pointy trigger-finger salutes to the headwaiter, which would normally be very Patrick Bateman in *American Psycho* but in this case is completely captivating.

He arrives at your table and you extend your hand. "So nice to meet you. I've heard great things," you say.

He tugs at the edge of his jacket and shuffles his feet, mumbling something inaudible. "Sorry, what was that?" you ask.

"Use your words or no dessert!" a passing waiter barks at him. He flinches and spits out, "Nice to meet you, too."

You look around the restaurant to see if anyone else noticed that bizarre exchange. Just as you begin to consider something might be up, Carter flashes a pair of baby blue eyes your way and your heart melts. He flags down the waiter and orders two of "the usual."

"Oh, 'the usual,' huh?" you repeat. "I like a man who takes charge."

As you place your hand on his, the waiter plops down two boxes of Crayola crayons. This, evidently, is "the usual."

Carter notices your perplexed expression and assures you: "Only the best when you're with me. This box is from 1994. A very good year."

"Women mature a little faster than men. That's what they always say, isn't it?" you silently remind yourself.

As Carter doodles what looks to be a space alien–pig hybrid monster on the back of his placemat, you can't help but ask, "What is it you do again?"

"I'm an investment banker."

Okay, so he's good with numbers. Sure, he seems a little off, but then again what single thirty-year-old guy doesn't have a little growing up to do, right? You thought he might be slow, but maybe it's just that he's slow to commit.

He flags the waiter down to order some Cheerios. "I'm ready for my snackie," Carter announces.

You decide you've seen enough. "I think it's time for me to go," you say, as you stand up to leave. "We don't seem to have as much in common as I thought we would."

"No!" he screams. You're convinced he's about to throw a tantrum. "Listen—we have more in common than you think. I've done my research on you. You go to the Natural History

Museum every Friday and I'm going through this phase where I like to pretend I'm a dinosaur. You run marathons and I just learned how to do cartwheels. You're fluent in French and I'm fluent in pig Latin. Ouyay areway eautifulbay. It means—"

You cut him off. "I know what it means. I went to summer camp."

"You are beautiful," he cries out, as you head for the exit. You allow yourself one final glance back at Carter's handsome, albeit very blank, face. He looks lost and lonely, unable to function without some sort of guidance. You sigh. You feel a tinge of guilt mixed with a motherly instinct to want to tuck him into bed or read him a book. Plus, he is *really* hot. You stop in your tracks.

"Would you like to come home with me tonight?" you ask, as you approach the table once more.

"Maybe. Do you have Pringles in your apartment?"

It is inexplicably the best sex of your life. ●

LATE TO MATURE

There are grown-ups with childish tendencies who generally have it together (a category which you most likely fall under) and then there is the Man Child. After your first interaction with the Man Child, you will feel so confident in your own maturity that you immediately go and take out a mortgage on a home and start saying very grown-up things like "Dow Jones" and "paint swatches."

Man Children are an epidemic. Behind even the most charming, well-manicured, gorgeous exterior can reside a bona fide futon-sleeping, mommy-loving, cereal-for-dinner-eating Man Child. Lazy, spoiled, and emotionally slow, they often wind up with the sort of girls who have a very "nurturing" nature. They lure women in with what is perceived as a cool, laid-back attitude and a goofy inability to focus on anything for very long. These guys are indulged until they regress past all major stages in life, and what you're left with is a boyfriend with the interests and personal hygiene of a teenager, the temper of a toddler, and the object permanence understanding of an infant.

Are You Dating a Man Child?

1. His answer to the question "What is your favorite part of your girlfriend's body?" would most likely be:

a Her beautiful, soulful eyes.

b The way her hair gently falls onto her perfect, silky shoulders.

c Tit-tays.

2. No meal with your man is complete without:

a A bottle of wine.

b Eye contact and engaging conversation.

c Crayons. So he can trace his hand on the placemat. (Pro Tip: If you add a beak, it's a turkey!)

3. You get into a disagreement. Your man responds by:

a Taking a walk around the block to cool down before returning to calmly present his side of things.

b Writing you a long email clearly detailing his emotions and feelings.

c Balling up his fists and hunching over quietly in a corner. His face is *really* red. Is he crying or pooping?

4. His idea of the perfect woman is:

a A goofy, down-to-earth girl, like Jennifer Lawrence.

b A sultry seductress, like Sofia Vergara.

c Someone who can roll a fat joint, like Snoop Dogg.

5. The movie he'll never get sick of watching is:

a *Citizen Kane* (The. Best. Movie. Ever. Made.)

b *The Big Lebowski* (He even took you bowling on your first date!)

c *Toy Story 2* (It's kind of his thing to say, "To infinity and beyond!" before having sex.)

6. When booking flights for your anniversary vacation, he goes straight to:

a Travelocity. (He loves a great deal!)

b His assistant. (What a high-powered business professional!)

c His mom.

7. His New Year's resolution this year was:

a To take a trip to Europe! He really wants to travel more.

b To volunteer more often. He wants to do something more meaningful with his Sundays.

c Going to the dentist for the first time in ten years. ("As long as they don't use the drill! Oh the drill! Not the drill! Make the drill go away! Please don't make me go! I don't want to go anymore.")

8. His group of friends most closely resembles:

a The cast of *Entourage*. The power players around town.

b The cast of *The Big Bang Theory*. All of the smarts minus the cheesy laugh track.

c The cast of *The Sandlot*. A lot of mischief, gawking at women in public pools, and puberty.

9. He'd like the first dance song at your wedding to be:

a Frank Sinatra's "The Way You Look Tonight" (Such a classic!)

b Rihanna's "We Found Love" (Oh, funky! Plus, you totally did.)

c "The Imperial March" (Perhaps more commonly known as Darth Vader's theme song, you noob.)

10. You knew he was "the one" the moment:

a You met him! He was a charmer from the start.

b He surprised you at work on your one-year anniversary. He's always so thoughtful.

c You saw him playing with your niece and nephew during Thanksgiving at the kids' table. He looked really in the zone, so much so that he moved his entire place setting there.

SCORE If you've answered "c" for more than four of the above questions, congrats, Mama! Looks like the stork swung by your pad and dropped off this 180-pound bundle of joy. Make sure to keep your kitchen well-stocked with Fruit Roll-Ups, hold his hand when crossing the street, and burn every wedding magazine you have ever purchased because, nope, that is not happening.

MORAL OF THE STORY **A FOOL AND HIS HUNNY ARE SOON PARTED**

You probably don't want to spend your life raising a Man Child. In some cases (mostly in movies produced by Judd Apatow), a good woman can show a Man Child the error of his foolish ways and he will eventually move past this temporary phase of life and get a good job and a haircut, and maybe learn some Very Valuable Lessons along the way. More likely, however, if you start dating a guy who still sleeps in a bunk bed at his parents' house, you'll find yourself tumbling from the top bunk two years later, breaking your femur, and cursing the day you ever met this guy. This is why entering into a relationship with the hope of changing a person is usually a bad move.

You certainly want to be honest with a guy about what you're looking for—but most importantly, be honest with yourself. You might be at the stage in your life where you're not all that worried about the future. The easygoing, non-committal, occasionally pot-smoking aspects of a Man Child might be exactly what you're looking for. In that case, you can ride off happily into the sunset with your Seth Rogen doppelgänger.

You Can't Get Over Your Ex

The Interviewer and the Applicants

A lobby full of bright-eyed young hopefuls sit outside your office. Some sweat, some adjust their tie, some adjust their junk. You try to sneak a peek at them. There's been a lot of pressure on you after the abrupt departure of the full-timer who last filled this post.

Today, you are interviewing candidates for the role of New Boyfriend. More accurately, you'd qualify this as falling in the Rebound Department. That's the department right across from HR. This role was previously inhabited by a four-year vet named Brendan, a well-respected pro (never forgot a birthday, gave a great foot massage), but now you're looking for someone entry-level. A new mind you can mold.

You should call in the first interviewee, but first you refresh your ex's LinkedIn profile one more time. If Brendan has found a new position with someone else, you will do this meeting high and in your pajamas. To your relief, Brendan is still unemployed.

You call in the first applicant. He saunters in, briefcase in hand. His strawberry-blond hair rises three inches above his forehead and he flashes a youthful grin. He is wearing an emerald tie, which is a nice touch. Maybe too nice. He's trying too hard, you decide.

"Hi, I'm Noah," he introduces himself, as you get up to greet him and alternate between a handshake and a hug, until you manage an awkward in-between maneuver in which you basically hug his wrists with your hands.

You scan the resume he has handed you. Noah lives with two roommates and held his last position for a solid eight months. Special skills include making smoothies, changing light bulbs, hanging up towels on the rack, and putting toilet paper over to under.

"Noah, why would you like to be a member of this team?" you ask.

"I was really impressed by the honesty of your mission statement. I even memorized it. 'To maintain a relationship that brings joy to all company personnel, makes the popular girls from high school who made fun of your unibrow jealous, qualifies you to give unsolicited dating advice to your single friends, and motivates your family to keep believing you will carry on their bloodline.'"

You might have been a little drunk when you wrote that mission statement.

"So, what do you like to do for fun?" he asks.

"I will open up questions at the end," you scold him. Who the hell does this joker think he is? Your ex Brendan would never be so brash. You are the boss and had better assert your dominance right here and now.

"What are your weaknesses?" you ask.

"I've been told I'm a perfectionist. I'm known to stay late at the office cuddling in bed and I've implemented a time management system to make sure I finish tasks before a deadline—purchasing anniversary gifts weeks in advance. I'm a workaholic!"

"I think I have all I need," you tell Noah. "But I'm going to need a few references other than your mother by EOD. *Now*, do you have any questions?"

"Well, I'd like to know what a typical day of being your boyfriend would be like?"

"What I need from you could change from week to week. The basics include prompt texts from you every morning to tell me to have a good day at work. You'd have to repeat this several times throughout the day, checking in on me. On an especially busy day you would also email me a funny article you came across so that I can read it on my lunch break. Are you familiar with using Instagram?"

"Yes, I would consider myself at an above-average proficiency level. I included that at the bottom of my resume, next to Word, Excel, PowerPoint, and Netflix."

"You'd use Instagram a lot with me," you say. "I like about two pictures posted a month featuring either just me or us together to subtly alert your friends and ex-girlfriends as to the happy and fun nature of our relationship. Does that answer your question?"

"I think so. Maybe I can call you sometime and we can do this again?" Noah says.

"I'll get back to you in about three to five business days and let you know if I'll need a follow-up interview."

You walk him out and he looks disappointed. Maybe you should have made out with him? You just don't know the procedure anymore. Why did Brendan have to leave and ruin everything? Replacing him feels impossible. If only you had kept things exciting and done something unexpected, like reinstating Bagel Fridays.

"Next!" you cry out.

A new guy named Oliver enters. He has a chiseled jawline and sultry brown eyes. His Tattersall-patterned button-up shirt is only half tucked in. You can't tell if it's on purpose or not, but hot damn, it looks good.

"Before I waste either of our time, I have a quick question," he tells you. "I see that this is an internship position. I was hoping for something long-term."

"Allow me to clarify," you say. "Occasionally an internship can lead to a full-time position. However, right now I do not have the emotional resources to settle on one permanent individual."

"I see," he says, as he hands you his resume.

Oliver owns his own apartment. He is fluent in all five Love Languages, plus basic Spanish. Special skills include hailing cabs, weekly calls to his mom, and making the bed.

"It looks like you've jumped around a lot with previous companies. What made you leave those positions before the three-month mark?"

"I realized I was wasting my time at startups that seemed like they were going to take off, but behind the scenes had spotty infrastructures and daddy issues," Oliver explains. "I'm looking for a company where I can grow and move up. I need a company that wants to invest in me."

Not a bad answer.

"Listen," you say. "Hundreds of hungry young men get off the bus every day here looking for a position just like this. It's a foot in the door. If that's not good enough for you, you might have to look elsewhere."

"I don't even care about great benefits," begs Oliver. "In my last situation, I didn't have any. No engaging conversations, no comforting when I'd had a stressful day, zero oral. I'm not in it for that. I may not have the experience but I have the drive."

He's got gumption, you'll give Oliver that. You start to think maybe Brendan is replaceable. You decide to make an offer.

"How do you feel about freelance?"

"Go on," Oliver answers, intrigued.

"A freelance position would be more secure than an internship. I'd take you a little more seriously, but you wouldn't be on call 24/7 like you would if you were a full-timer. We'd both be invested but it's still sort of a trial thing. How would that work for you?"

He smiles. "I'll take the gig!"

You tell the rest of the guys in the waiting room to go home, but you hold on to their resumes. You know, in case this freelancer doesn't work out. ●

THE RECOVERY PERIOD

How long it takes to get over an ex will vary for everybody. No matter who did the breaking—you or him—it can take some time for you to recover.

Being in a relationship is like creating your own little country that has its own language and customs and a strict immigration policy. Once you depart from this jointly founded couple country, you need to adapt and deal with your culture shock. It is wise to take your time when it comes to meeting a new person because your brain is still running on couple-country time. You need to wait to get over jet lag.

However, if your breakup occurred so long ago that, for example, there's an entirely new cast on *Saturday Night Live* and at least two of the old cast members have made a smooth transition into film, you are probably staying a bit too long at the pity party.

Application for New Boyfriend

NAME

Pete Howell

ARE YOU ELIGIBLE TO DATE? (PLEASE SPECIFY IF YOU ARE IN ANY WAY "ATTACHED," "ON A BREAK," OR ENGAGING IN SOMETHING "COMPLICATED")

I subscribe to the "hoes in different area codes" philosophy, so I am currently ineligible in the 212, 424, 414, 512, 714, and 564 regions. I am available and eager everywhere else!

PREVIOUS RELATIONSHIP DUTIES

Expertly paid for most meals, diligently learned the names and interests of all close friends, provided excellent emotional support, collated all old texts from ex-girlfriends and deleted them in a timely manner.

REASON FOR ENDING LAST RELATIONSHIP?

Creative differences, plus she was a bitch.

WHY ARE YOU INTERESTED IN THIS RELATIONSHIP?

I have a lot of weddings coming up and I am very interested in the thought of a permanent plus-one.

HOW DID YOU LEARN ABOUT THIS OPENING?

Your mom is friends with my mom and told her you've been real depressed lately. Seemed like a great opportunity.

CERTIFICATIONS

A "Birth Certificate" from Build-A-Bear, issued February 13 of last year. I'm a very thoughtful gift-giver.

TIMES AND DAYS AVAILABLE FOR DATES

I am interested in mid-week hangs and would be available most weekends, though keeping Wednesdays, Thursdays, Fridays, and Sundays open is preferred.

SOCIAL SECURITY NUMBER

Is this really necessary?

PERMISSION TO CONTACT PAST GIRLFRIENDS?

~~Yes, no restraining orders!~~ Yes, you can contact them!

IS ALL THE INFORMATION YOU HAVE SUPPLIED ACCURATE?

Yes. Well, full disclosure: my little sister helped me build that bear, but I picked out his tuxedo!

MORAL OF THE STORY THE LONGER YOU LIVE IN THE PAST, THE LESS FUTURE HOTTIES YOU HAVE TO ENJOY

What will help you tremendously is ridding yourself of any past remnants of your ex.

- Don't see each other for a long time after breaking up.
- Block him on Facebook, unfollow his Twitter and Instagram, unSnap his Chat, and unwind his Vine.
- Don't show up at places because you think he will be there.
- If you have mutual friends, don't grill them for information.
- In time, you two may be able to "be friends," but in the immediate future "being friends" is going to wind up being code for "hook up occasionally and cry when he eventually gets a new girlfriend, which he is totally free to do since you are both single." It's called a post-relationship relationship and it happens every time.

You may think you're simply being friendly by keeping the social media lines open with your ex. But the less you know, the better. It's the only way to move on.

TIWYS

You're in the Friend Zone

The Crush and the Pal

Neil is everything you ever wanted in a guy. He likes sports, but not obsessively. He fixes anything that goes wrong in his apartment instead of calling the super. His hair always looks handsomely disheveled, but you know he doesn't try. He's kind. He's creative. He's respectful—has never made a move the entire time you've known him.

You meet him at his apartment for post-work dinner one night. He's offered to cook, which you take to be an excellent sign. Everyone knows there is only one reason a man cooks: to impress a woman. Well, that, and to feed himself when he's hungry. You arrive in a new dress, heels, and makeup you have reapplied at least twice on your way over. Neil answers the door in sweats and a ripped shirt with what appears to be permanent pit stains under each arm.

"Hey there, Emeril!" you quip.

He lets out a burp and welcomes you inside his unkempt apartment.

Some people might read these to be signs that Neil isn't concerned about impressing you, but you think you know what's really going on here. He is *so* comfortable with you! This is the kind of intimacy it takes most people years to establish.

"So I've been meaning to talk to you about something," he says, as he plops onto his worn-down futon. "But I didn't know how to ask you."

You knew it! All of those times Neil coyly tried to play dumb about your interest in him were just because he was afraid to feel true emotion. The emotion he felt about you.

"It's a bit of a commitment," he adds.

Talk about a 180! You did not anticipate this kind of bluntness. You always hated those jerkoffs that gush about "marrying their best friend," but now you get to be one of those jerkoffs. You re-focus your attention on Neil so you don't miss a word of this milestone moment.

"And things can tend to get a little aggressive in the heat of the moment. I've even been known to use some rough language."

Is Neil talking about in the bedroom? Already?! Little does he know you've always gone for the dirty-talk thing.

You lean toward him and in a seductive voice whisper, "Bring it on."

"Great! You better start thinking of a team name!" he says.

A team. A partnership. A united front. That's how he sees you two and that is how you shall evermore be known. You try to brainstorm and think back on some of your other favorite team names: "Brangelina," "Bennifer," "Jelly Prevolta."

"I'm going to need some time to think of the perfect one," you tell him.

"Wow, you're taking this so seriously already. You're going to be great in fantasy."

In fantasy? Does he mean in *his* fantasies? In his fantasies about your future together? But . . . fantasy has become reality, right?

"I wasn't even sure if you watched football," he says. "Guess I should listen more when you talk. Welcome to our fantasy league!"

Wait—league? Oh my god. He's talking about fantasy football. This entire time you've been imagining what a baby might look like with your ski slope nose and his luscious eyelashes, he's been imagining what sort of players you would put on a fake sports team lineup? IS ANYTHING REAL ANYMORE?

You play everything through your head like a movie flashback. That time you picked him up from the bar when he had too much to drink. That time he built all of your IKEA furniture when you moved into a new apartment. All of those weeks playing together on a co-ed soccer team. The fact that you are on a first-name basis with his entire family. You are a couple that has always been there for one another. And by "couple," you mean a couple of besties. You're like a sister to him. No, worse. You're just one of his bros. ●

GETTING IN THE ZONE

Platonic male and female friendships are 100% real and happen all the time. Anyone who says any different is a dumb liar or Harry in *When Harry Met Sally* . . . However, on occasion, warm and fuzzy feelings might arise and this is when things get complicated.

There are different ways to unintentionally enter into the zone that is friend:

- You may start out as friends and develop feelings later (so much later that you are now past the point of no return and are thought to be genderless).

- You may have feelings right away and see friendship as an easy "in" to romance. Not a bad idea, but if you do too convincing a job of just wanting to be pals you can friend-zone yourself.

- You may have already expressed interest in a person and been directly told that he feels you are "better off" as friends. You accept this idea because you just want to be close to this perfect specimen, but deep down you are harboring the secret belief that if you two sit through enough Manny Pacquiao boxing matches together, eventually magic will happen.

MORAL OF THE STORY **IF YOU DON'T ASK, THE ANSWER IS ALWAYS "ZONED!"**

If you are convinced there is potential for love in this buddy-comedy-turned-horror-flick that is your life, then your best option is to tell him how you feel. This could potentially ruin your friendship, but then again, so could the repressed, *Carrie*-like anger bubbling inside of you each time you hear him talk about another girl. This conversation will set your mind at ease knowing that your feelings are out there, not to mention prevent you from murdering a bunch of people through a rage-fueled telekinetic outburst.

CLASSIC EPISODES OF *THE FRIEND ZONE*

Cue creepy music and floating clocks in space. Do-do-do-do-do-do-do-do

"Eye of the Beholder"

We meet a woman wrapped in bandages, in a hospital. She has just undergone a surgery that will make her look like the type of girl her *friend* has always gone for. When she reveals herself to him, it turns out he is now dating a girl who looks just like the woman did before her surgery. Guess it wasn't her looks he wasn't into, just her personality! Oh well, back to the drawing board. Also, everyone has a pig face.

"Nightmare at 20,000 Feet"

A man sits uneasily in the middle seat of an airplane. He asks his *friend* in the window seat to switch and she adoringly obliges. He proceeds to fall asleep with his head on her shoulder and whispers, "You're the best." The friend is convinced the man has feelings for her. The plane lands and the man immediately turns on his phone to call his girlfriend. The friend proceeds to turn into a gremlin and claw the wing of the plane with her bare hands in anger as she exits. She still offers to drop the man off at his beautiful girlfriend's house.

"Frozen in Time"

A pretty girl excitedly preps for a dinner date with her *friend*. She shows up only to find there are four other dudes at the Mexican restaurant. Though there are many opportunities for this pack of bros to leave, none of them do. The evening never ends and no one ever leaves and everyone is stuck perpetually in an awkward group hang . . . until the end of time.

"Living Doll"

A sweet young lady receives a Talky Tina doll (a bootleg version of Chatty Cathy) as a gift from her mother to cheer her up after years of unrequited love from her *friend*. Although the doll is meant to lift her spirits, it says evil things when you pull the string on its back. "My name is Talky Tina. You know he intentionally changes the subject whenever you bring up soulmates, right?" and "My name is Talky Tina. He would rather go home alone and jerk off than have sex with you." The episode ends with Talky Tina at the bottom of a flaming garbage can.

You Mix Business with Pleasure

The Elf and Santa

It's winter break and you've picked up the oddest of odd jobs. Dressed from head to toe in red and green felt and jingling at every step you take, you are in a decidedly unsexy situation. Nothing says "desperate to pick up a little extra holiday cash" like a pair of pointy elf shoes and a name tag that says, "Hi, My Name is Jingleberry!"

Much to your surprise though, about a week into your gig as Santa's helper at the mall, you get into a merry mood. Coming to work every day isn't so bad when you and Saint Nick develop a will-they-or-won't-they vibe that rivals Ross and Rachel season four (the one with British Emily). It turns out you and Santa Claus are extremely sextually compatible. It should be noted that this Santa Claus does not have his AARP card, is only a few years older than you, has six-pack abs, and an eight-inch dick. He got the gig when the elderly Santa dropped dead of a heart attack around Thanksgiving (RIP old Santa).

Keeping your love a secret feels great . . . because it feels naughty. The use of the word *naughty* when your boyfriend is a Mall Santa is not something you're proud to admit is a strangely big turn-on. However, one day you walk into the reindeer shed an hour before the mall opens and discover Santa rolling around in the hay with two skanks from Sbarro.

You're devastated, but the show must go on. This is the difficult thing about canoodling with a co-worker—you must remain professional. After all, it's only a week before Christmas and there are two hundred children lined up.

You show up to work the next day vowing to behave like a grown-up and entertain his strained attempts at small talk.

"So, how was your weeken—"

"You are scum," you respond.

You take a breath and compose yourself as a sweet little six-year-old girl in pigtails and a red dress approaches. You want to tell her that life is a stagnant bucket of lies and we're all drowning in it, but instead you say, "Welcome to the North Pole!" as you plop the little girl on Santa's lap, a lap that you used to hump.

"Ho-ho-ho! Merry Christmas!" welcomes Santa. "What do you want for Christmas, little girl?"

"A puppy!" she squeals, clapping her hands.

"A puppy?" Santa exclaims. "You know, that's a lot of commitment!"

You try to keep your lips sealed but the words involuntarily fall out.

"That's right! And Santa doesn't like commitment. *Do you*, Santa?"

So much for maturity. Get your head in the game, elf girl.

"Ho-ho-ho! Do you think you are old enough to take care of a puppy?" Santa asks, changing the subject away from his commitment issues (as per usual).

You jump in, channeling the joy and spunk of Buddy the Elf. "Well gee golly, Santa! That question isn't really fair. Cause sometimes your birth certificate can say you're a certain age, but then you don't act that age at all!" You pause for dramatic emphasis, staring deep into Santa's eyes. "For example, Santa is centuries old but instead of enjoying his stable, merry, grown-up life in the North Pole, Santa just looks for the next best thing. Like a baby."

Just when you're about to give over to the ugly-crys, your manager strolls by. You need that paycheck ('tis the season!) so you hold it together.

"Uh, yes, Santa is young at heart," he stammers, before going in for the kill. "You know, little girl, puppies seem like a great idea when you see them sleeping like little angels. But then they keep you up all night with their barking and their yapping and they try to bring you to couples therapy."

"What?" the little girl asks.

"Uh, sometimes puppies are too emotional."

"What?!" you scream.

"I bet you think you're gonna love that puppy forever, huh?" Santa continues.

"Yes, forever!" the little girl assures him.

He looks down at her. "Forever is a very, very, *very* long time."

Santa is an emotional terrorist! You try to hold it together, but when the next child asks Santa for LEGOs, you lose it.

"Oh, you want to build things with your LEGOs, do you?" you cry, as you begin chucking Christmas ornaments at Santa and drop-kicking presents. "I wanted to build something once, too. Do you know what I wanted to build? A future! Some-times you build a beautiful tower with your LEGOs and then you find Santa screwing a pizza slut and it all comes crashing down!"

You are promptly let go from your job and banned from the mall for a year. ●

OFFICE ROMANCE

Even if you are one of those people who "love what you do," there are still going to be mornings when your alarm goes off and you question all the choices that have led you to this moment. You might even consider rolling out of bed and dragging your body into oncoming traffic. Eventually you have a cup of coffee and snap out of it. But coffee only goes so far. What you really need to get you to the office on time and feeling perky is a work crush. When you have a work crush, you look forward to your nine-to-five. That's eight straight hours of stolen glances and flirty emails on the clock.

Once you two take things from platonic to physical (office party make-out, carpool dry-hump, storage closet quickie), it is past the point of no return. Things can go from exciting to awkward pretty quickly. For starters, you'll probably want to keep your tryst a secret until you figure out if it's more than just a fling. That means lots of Monday morning meetings with weird sexual tension that really confuses your disgruntled fifty-year-old boss. Eventually you show up to work wearing the same clothing from the day before, people catch on, and rumors start flying that the only reason you loaned him your stapler long-term is because he gave you a couple of boob hickeys over Labor Day weekend. You don't really care though, because you're having a ton of fun.

However, a happy relationship is far easier to hide and/or deny to HR than a toxic one. When things start to implode, suddenly an argument about how to properly load paper into the copy machine is taken personally, and soon you are bawling in your cubicle and maniacally ripping pictures from the company camping trip off the wall because they remind you of happier times. You are distracted and moody, which are actually pretty normal emotions to have at work, except that instead of absentmindedly checking your Facebook to avoid productivity, you're obsessively checking his Facebook to watch his every move.

MORAL OF THE STORY ## ONE WOMAN'S MATE IS ANOTHER WOMAN'S CO-WORKER

This means when you're sitting at home and a co-worker comes up on a dating app, you must follow the appropriate steps:

1. Scream in horror

2. Screenshot his profile and send it to your best work friend

3. Ask yourself these three questions:

> 1. Is he in your department? 2. Is he your boss? 3. Are you his boss?

If you answered yes to any of these three questions, ex out and don't bring it up with him. There are plenty of other potential hookups a finger flick away. Don't get tangled up with a relationship that could negatively affect your career. If you answered no to all three questions and you think your day-to-day life at the company could survive the worst possible breakup scenario, then go ahead and let the messaging begin! But beware: While a midday lunch smooch is cute, nothing kills the divine powers of a workplace infatuation quicker than going on a date and getting to know all the mundane details that downgrade a celestial crush to a mere mortal.

When Everyone Knows You're Dating

You think you both are playing it so cool, but everything you say is simply saturated in sexual innuendo.

What You Say	What Your Co-Workers Hear
"Can I expect the project by noon?"	"Can I expect to get some poon?"
"We're going to Starbucks!"	"We're going to car fuck!"
"Send that contract over to me."	"I have contracted an STD."
"You got the promotion!"	"You got the lotion?"
"I think the problem is the modem."	"I think the problem is your scrotum."

You're in Love with Your Gay BFF

The Prince and the Princess

You live for your slumber parties with Steven. Your tastes are so compatible—John Waters flicks, *Scandal* marathons, late '80s Whitney, and early '90s Mariah. You can talk about anything, from your insecurities to your hopes and dreams to sexual tips and tricks (you have Steven to thank for your signature move: the Upside-Down Walrus). Steven even took your advice and got one of your favorite haircuts on a guy—the Fade/Ivy League hybrid. You laugh at all his jokes and he doesn't judge you for drinking Pinot Grigio like someone's middle-aged aunt.

Gosh, Steven is perfect.

You take a gulp of your Pinot, this time straight from the box.

"Woah, when was the last time you ate something?" he asks you.

He is so caring. He will make a great father someday. And unlike some of your other guy friends (the straight ones), you know his concern for you comes from his heart and isn't motivated by some lustful secret fantasy to screw you. You know this because Steven screws men, not ladies.

You plop your head on Steven's shoulder. "You always smell so good," you slur.

You are in love with Steven, and, god, how tragic it is that you were born with female genitalia. In the time it takes him to discreetly inch away from your drunk bobble-head, you've come to the conclusion that, logic be damned, tonight is the night you'll make your move on your soulmate.

"Wouldn't it be crazy if we just made out right now?" you ask, trying to sound casual and fun.

"What is it about cheap Trader Joe's wine that gets you so wet?" he says. "Girl, you need to get laid."

He has no idea.

"Have you ever given any thought to the idea of sexuality being . . . fluid?" you ask.

He rolls his eyes. You try again.

"Haven't you ever wondered what a vagina feels like?"

"Sure, but I've also wondered what it would feel like to stick a fork in an electrical socket."

You work another angle.

"Would it help if I tell you I haven't really shaved my legs in a while? I honestly probably feel like a dude right now."

"I grappled throughout my entire adolescence with my sexuality and can tell you for a fact, your hairy lady legs are not gonna get me hard," Steven replies, as he gathers up his things to leave. "I'll talk to you tomorrow."

"I know what this is about," you say. "You're a bottom. Ugh. Fine. I'll try a strap-on."

"What the fuck is wrong with you?" he screams.

Uh-oh. There goes your perfect evening together! You try to salvage things.

"Wait! Don't go. Let's just chill out and watch *Valley of the Dolls* with director commentary turned on."

He slams the door.

The truth is, you can't blame the booze for your horrible behavior. You can trace your preference for fun and flamboyant men all the way back to your childhood.

You lay your head down on your box of wine and think back to your eight-year-old self, playing alone in your childhood bedroom. Barbies were strewn about and you can clearly remember the sort of shit you had spewing out of Prince Ken's mouth to Rapunzel Barbie.

"Rapunzel, Rapunzel!" you lisped while shaking Prince Ken in Rapunzel Barbie's face. "I *seriously* cannot get over this hair. Do you condition or is this just natural?"

This made-up dream man of yours was so dashing and detail-oriented. Rapunzel Barbie unraveled her long, ratty Barbie weave down to the prince to climb.

"You want me to *climb* your hair? Are you freaking crazy? And ruin it? No!" he cried. "Literally the most important thing I will ever say to you: omega-3 vitamins and no hair climbing."

Some princes wouldn't mind being seen in public with an unkempt princess, but he would never.

"Look, homegurl," Prince Ken declared. "Cinderella's Ball is tonight. Why don't you just run your cute little tush down here and we can go togeth? I just wanna dance! Don't you ever just, like, wanna dance?"

Rapunzel Barbie was delighted to attend her very first ball with her one true love. Once she was dressed, this charming prince heroically exclaimed, "OMG, you look fierce. You are so putting Cinderella to shame at her own party. PS, I heard she turns into a total slut at midnight."

"Prince Ken, you're such a little bitch!" Rapunzel Barbie squeaked.

The game you played always ended the same way: Rapunzel Barbie and Prince Ken decided they were soulmates. They happily wed and had lots and lots of babies.

In reality, your present-day fairy tale has a very different ending. After years of spending your weekends with the sort of guys who would rather braid your hair than bump your nasty, your gay BFF finds a serious boyfriend and you become the unfortunate third wheel in *his* romantic fairy tale. They (that is, your gay best friend Steven and his boyfriend Stephen) live happily ever after. ●

GAY BFFS MAKE GREAT . . . FRIENDS

Where did these childhood preferences originate? For one, Disney has lied to you. No straight man has an eye for unique footwear like Prince Charming. No hetero guy is down to sing some fabulous duet on the first date *à la* Prince Phillip in *Sleeping Beauty.* As for *Tiger Beat,* they encouraged lots of preteen fantasies involving Ricky Martin, Lance Bass, and the Hanson brothers. (Okay, the Hansons aren't gay but they *are* super Christian and got hitched pretty early on, so they were not a viable option in the marriage department either.) While you may be nostalgic for your childhood, it's time to update your sexual preferences.

Your friendship with your GBFF is one you should cherish. The fierce alliance between gay men and straight, single women is one that rivals the allegiance between America and England, Daria Morgendorffer and Jane Lane, and Richard Hatch and whoever else was on *Survivor* season one. They need each other. Both groups have a history of misrepresentation and misplaced shame and have struggled to find acceptance in the world. Both have fended off unflattering stereotypes and are now having what some might consider "a moment." The instinct to clink glasses and cheers to their shared good fortune has taken this bond to the next level. There is a real comfort level to these friendships.

But woe unto that sad sort of girl who confuses her relationship with this loyal fellow as anything other than BFF status. Let's face it, even though your head recognizes that your gay BFF knows every word to *The Rocky Horror Picture Show* and dresses better than you do, the heart is stubborn and just wants someone to big spoon you while you watch *Dirty Dancing,* which sometimes he totally does.

MORAL OF THE STORY

ATTEMPT NOT UN-FUCKABILITIES

If you'd like to avoid suffering this sad but far too common romantic fate, you can start by remembering:

1. When the Stev(ph)ens bump and grind with you on the dance floor, it is purely platonic.

2. Your childhood expectations were misguided.

3. Cut back on the Pinot.

REASONS YOU WANT TO MARRY YOUR GAY BFF

1. He smells good.

2. He reacts the exact same way you do when Britney Spears's song "Lucky" comes on.

3. You would have the best-dressed wedding guests ever.

4. He knows all of your secrets.

5. You've already taken dance classes together.

6. You never feel pressured to have sex with him when you're tired (or anytime for that matter).

7. His pop cultural intellect is astonishingly impressive.

8. You hate all of the same people.

REASONS YOU CAN'T MARRY HIM

1. He is not sexually or romantically attracted to you in any way.

gaydar \ gādär \ *n* **1 :** The ability to identify if somebody is gay or straight based on purely superficial observations and stereotypes. Certain factors, mainly British accents, are known to throw off a person's gaydar. Often, hetero men with the various talents typically associated with gay men (fantastic dancing, being well-groomed, having a gorgeous singing voice, being an Academy Award–winning actor, having a liberal intellect, and throwing a fabulous dinner party) are confused with being gay. In this case, it is a compliment to both the gays and the talented hetero. Falling in love with your gay best friend is different from having bad gaydar.

You Keep Going on Bad Dates

The Loser and the Lady

Here you are. The ultimate trial. A face-to-face, one-on-one dinner date. There's no loud music. No chatty friends to distract you. No drunk guy at the bar yelling, "Get your drink on and your dick out!" to band together against. No bouncer telling everyone to leave before the convo gets stale. No trivial viral YouTube video of a baby playing with a squirrel to send him that substitutes you having to be funny over email. No *Atlantic* think piece on gentrification you can message over to show him you're socially conscious. There is nothing between the two of you but some overpriced tilapia. It's like staring down the barrel of a candlelit gun.

The previous day, you went to H&M, bought six different sweater-skirt combos, and sent your friends outfit selfies so they could help you decide which one to wear (all six friends chose a different outfit so you went with something you already owned. But that's beside the point). You went into work an hour early so you could sneak out early (which you made sure to announce to your co-workers multiple times throughout the day with a "Can you believe it's dark at 7 A.M.? I would know. Because I was at work."). You sprayed perfume in all of those places they do in Chanel No. 5 commercials (those models spray their crotches too, right?).

Hopes are high and the excitement of your anticipation makes you feel like a kid on Christmas morning. Except for that Christmas morning when all you wanted was a Puppy Surprise doll (the surprise being that your stuffed animal was knocked up) but instead awoke to find Baby Bop–themed thermal underwear under the tree. That's what this date is. Thermal-underwear-from-Santa-on-Christmas-morning level bad.

"My ex-girlfriend had that coat," is your date Max's suave opening line.

Throughout the course of the evening, Max will bring up this particular ex no less than fifteen times and will use descriptors ranging from "sexual Olympian" to "crazy" to "my grandmother told me to marry her on her deathbed" when discussing her.

Max's dating profile said he was 6'0" but he's 5'5" at the most. His too-tight dad jeans have given him a girl-like bubble butt and he's chosen to wear a faded cotton T-shirt from Kid Rock's "Lazy Muthafuga" tour. You're not sure if it's acne or a herpes cold sore outbreak on his lower lip, but it takes all of your willpower not to stare at it.

After a rocky start, the waiter comes over and eases the stiff atmosphere.

"Some water to start?"

"Sure! Tap is fine for me," you say.

"Who the fuck does that guy think he is?" Max asks after the waiter has left.

As a question such as this is usually rhetorical, you do not answer.

"He was totally flirting with you!" he accuses.

You attempt to defuse this particular crazy bomb with an adorable joke about how you only order wine that tastes like juice.

"Why don't you just order grape juice then?" he replies.

Do you know that feeling when a joke is lost in translation but you both speak English? It's that. The waiter returns.

"Have you had a chance to look at the menus yet?" he asks.

"I'm going to kill him," Max whispers to you across the table.

"We're going to need a few more seconds," you say to the waiter.

Aggressive and jealous tendencies? Check. Hung up on an ex? Check. You're stuck here until the what? Check.

You attempt some small talk.

"What's your, uh, favorite movie?" you ask him.

"I don't have one," he replies.

You try again.

"What do you do for a living?"

"I don't have one."

It feels like four hours but it's actually only forty minutes later when the date is over and you are free to leave. You slip the waiter a twenty after Max announces it's insane waiters expect anything more than 7% gratuity. You assume it has been mutually decided that there is zero chemistry and that this was a very bad date by any standard.

You return to the safety of your home and padlock the door behind you, relieved to have escaped the nightmare of a date. A few minutes later you get a text from Max. "We should do that again sometime." ●

GETTING DUPED

A guy might seem great on paper, but then you meet him and realize it was all a sham. It's the equivalent of that time you saw a really bad psychic and found yourself giving him the benefit of the doubt just because you wanted the experience to be real. "Your brother is in danger!" the psychic told you. You're an only child so you thought, "Okay, he must mean my *metaphorical* brother. I am really close with my neighbor. I must warn him!" It's easy to cut someone some slack because you want the experience to be worthwhile.

Whether it's through mutual friends, online, or in the corner bodega, you tend to see people through Valencia-colored filters if they are cute enough and you see a morsel of romantic potential. You are first introduced to him putting his "best foot" forward, but that is quickly followed by a first-date introduction to his "horrible deformed smelly club foot."

Disaster Date Drinking Game

Turn that bad date into a winner! Because who can have a bad time when you're drunk on someone else's tab (unless you end up with the bill—but don't worry, there's points for that too!)?

> **WARNING: The creators of this game are not responsible for side effects such as headaches, slurred speech, drooling, nip slips, and, in the case of an extremely awful date, alcohol poisoning and death. Play with discretion.**

The Rules

Take a whiskey shot every time he:

- Mentions an ex
- Alludes to mommy issues
- Has a weird eye twitch
- Asks if you have any hot friends
- Uses a napkin as a bib
- Subtly mentions he's living at home
- Subtly mentions his six-figure income
- Subtly mentions how he dated a former reality show contestant
- Takes a whiskey shot

Chug some beer if you:

- Notice he's wearing dad jeans
- Are experiencing this date in a Chick-fil-A
- Are experiencing this date in an Applebee's
- Are pretty sure he has no idea what your first name is
- Realize you've had something in your teeth for the last fifteen minutes and don't care
- Fall asleep with your eyes open

Take a tequila shot if he admits he:

- Has never loved another person
- Has never voted
- Thinks Washington, D.C. is in the state of Washington

Throw a ping-pong ball into a glass on a nearby table every time:

- You realize there is a cute guy at a nearby table and want to get his attention
- You need to signal an outsider for help

Shoot heroin into your eyeball if:

- You get stuck with the bill

MORAL OF THE STORY — EVERYONE IS MORE OR LESS A MASTER OF HER OWN DATE

If you find yourself continuing to go on bad dates, look for a pattern. This could be a pattern in how you are meeting guys or in the type of guy you are going for. Once you have identified that pattern, break it. It's all trial and error. After all, the only way to tell the difference between an egg white substitute and a truffle mushroom frittata is to date a bunch of boxed egg white substitutes first. (If you are vegan, reverse this analogy. Same message.) So don't get down after a bad date, it will help you appreciate a good date all the more. Try all different kinds of egg dishes, but eventually, learn to stop ordering the ones that give you explosive diarrhea. *Bon appétit*!

Typical Bad Date Conversation

Most bad dates follow a similar structure. Fill in the blanks to re-create your own personalized disappointing exchange.

Guy: Wow, _____, you aren't as _____ as I
                     YOUR FIRST NAME   ADJECTIVE

thought you would be from looking at your profile.

You: Um, _____?
                      PLURAL NOUN

Guy: I hope you like this restaurant called _____
                                                                              ANY FRENCH WORD

et _____. I read all about it in
        ANY OTHER FRENCH WORD

_____.
              PRETENTIOUS MAGAZINE

You: _____!
                   ADJECTIVE

(A beat of awkward silence)

You: So, what do you do for fun?

Guy: I don't actually own a _____ so I spend a lot
                                                   BASIC HUMAN APPLIANCE

of time _____ my own _____ store on
               VERB ENDING IN "ING"   DIY PROJECT

Etsy and about _____ hours a day on _____.
                             NUMBER   LISTICLE-HEAVY WEBSITE

You: That sounds so _____. How did you wind up
                                           ADJECTIVE

on _____?
          DATING WEBSITE

Guy: I've been single for about _____ years now and
                                                          NUMBER

my _____ told me I had better act _____
          FAMILY MEMBER   ADJECTIVE

or I would never find anyone to marry me and I'd be living in his/

her _____ forever eating _____ from
            ROOM IN A HOUSE   FOOD

a _____.
          NOUN

You: Is that so?

Guy: Yeah. Guess it takes a special lady to go for a guy with an extensive _____ collection and four

NOUN

pet _____.

ANIMAL (PLURAL)

You: You're making me feel really _____.

ADJECTIVE

Guy: Maybe that's because you're a _____.

DEROGATORY WORD

You: Excuse me?!

Guy: Oh, sorry, I think you misunderstood me. I said

_____.

WORD THAT RHYMES WITH PREVIOUS DEROGATORY WORD

You: Right. You know, it's getting really late and I just remembered

I promised my _____ I would help him/

PERSON

her _____his/her _____. I should

VERB NOUN

get going.

Guy: That's too bad. Maybe we can get together another time and

you can let me _____ your _____

VERB BODY PART

and _____ your asshole.

VERB

You: Oh. My. _____.

DEITY

GO-TO EXCUSES TO LEAVE A DATE EARLY

1. My roommate is having a funeral tonight for our fern that died. Peace out!

2. I forgot to take my schizophrenia medication. "Shut up, Carla!" "No, you shut up!" *Ciao!*

3. I'm trying to win this scavenger hunt. Thanks for knocking "dinner with a stranger" off the list. Bye!

4. My dog has a date with another dog. See ya!

5. I have a lot of work to catch up on—fourteen shows on Netflix, Amazon, Vimeo, and DVR. *Hasta luego!*

6. Jimmy Choo has an online sale that starts at midnight. Ta-ta!

7. I know this ankle bracelet looks like a Fitbit, but I'm actually on house arrest. Cheerio!

8. I accidentally called myself an Uber. I'd cancel but I don't want to get charged. Farewell!

9. I mistakenly scheduled another date back-to-back. My bad. *Au revoir!*

10. I'm a Scientologist and I need to perform my nightly purification ritual against Xenu. So long!

SO YOU'RE DATING

You're Obsessed with Relationship Labels

The Robber and the Romance

It's time for date number four with Charlie. You aren't sure exactly what you two "are" yet but you think it's going somewhere. You like this one. You hope to get a definitive answer on just what exactly it is that you're "doing here" soon. What is "*this*"? Even for the sake of simple introductions alone, some clarity on this subject would be helpful.

Your buzzer rings and you head downstairs to go meet your . . . man . . . friend . . . with benefits . . . ?

"Hey, sweetie!" says Charlie as he plants a kiss on your forehead. The forehead is a sacred zone reserved for grandmas, your facialist, and boyfriends, so you take this to be a positive sign.

"Would you mind if we make a quick stop at the ATM?" he asks. "I was thinking we could walk through the farmers' market to get some hot apple cider before dinner. The hippie orchard lady only takes cash."

Mind? Of course not. Everyone knows that a vodka tonic is the drink of a hookup and an apple cider is the drink of longevity. This is great!

The ATM is down, so you and Charlie head over to the teller, a bored, middle-aged woman with big hair and a beige blazer. You have barely reached the teller's window when you hear the wheels of a car screech to a halt outside. The front door of the bank slams open and a towering man in a black turtleneck and a black ski mask over his face storms in, brandishing a silver pistol in the air.

You reflexively shriek.

"Okay, nobody move! This is a holdup," he shouts. "I'm taking all the fucking money in this place."

Do people still rob banks? Is this the Wild West? You begin to hyperventilate.

"Hey, you!" the robber shouts as he makes a beeline for Charlie. "Yeah, you and your little girlfriend. Get over here and shut up!"

Did he just say what you think he said? The robber called you Charlie's girlfriend and Charlie didn't correct him. This is huge!

The robber grabs you both by the arms and shoves you into a corner. Charlie crouches down beside you and throws a protective arm over your shoulders.

"Oh my god. Oh my god. Oh my god," you cry over and over.

"It'll be okay. Calm down," Charlie whispers.

"Girlfriend?" you whisper back.

"Huh?"

You stare up at him while the teller begins handing the robber stacks of money by the thousands, just a few feet away.

"That man just called me your girlfriend and you didn't correct him."

You knew tonight would be the night you finally got some answers. Charlie looks at you dumbstruck. Maybe he thinks you already knew you were both exclusive? That could be what's going on here.

The robber paces frantically back and forth, attempting to figure out his getaway plan on the fly. "I'll take the cash and go to Rio. Yeah, Rio. They'll never find me there. I'll open up a tiki bar, meet a nice half-naked girl at Carnival. Yeah . . . "

Charlie stays frozen as he searches for the right words.

"We're probably about to be murder—"

"Hey, didn't I tell you two to be quiet?" the robber snaps as he waves his gun in Charlie's face. "I have no qualms about killing every single person in here."

The teller lets out a fearful sob as Charlie assures the robber, "We'll be quiet. We're sorry."

"*We*? Are we a *we* now?" you ask.

Charlie holds up a finger to his mouth. Oh right, *we* are supposed to be quiet. Since Charlie still hasn't given you a direct response, you decide to give the definitive "what are we" Litmus Test with a nonverbal answer option.

"I'm scared," you whisper to Charlie. "Hold my hand."

Charlie grabs your hand . . . *in public*. Sirens wail in the distance as the robber makes a run for it out the front door.

Hours later, grateful to be alive, you, Charlie, and the teller sit inside a police station waiting to give statements.

"Do you mind if I just take a moment to call my mom?" you ask the officer. "I've had a really crazy day."

"Of course not, ma'am," the officer says.

"Hi, Mom," you say in a shaky voice when she picks up in less than half a ring. She's been trying to reach you for hours. ". . . Yeah, I figured you saw the news."

The news your mom is referring to, of course, is the evening news on which your face is plastered as a recently freed hostage of a local bank heist. You assume she means your now-updated relationship status on Facebook.

"Of course I'm okay," you tell her. "I have a boyfrienddddddd!" ●

PRE-RELATIONSHIP LIMBO

When it comes to romance, the right guy can turn even the coolest of cool chicks into a raving, insecure lunatic. You're great in every other way: Maybe you got a huge bonus at work, you're one of those girls who can wear a baseball cap and still look good, or you have the wittiest Wi-Fi network name on the block. But once you meet that special someone and hit what you perceive to be the "make it or break it" point, suddenly your mantra from the time you open your eyes in the morning until you rest your head on your pillow at night is a constant "WHAT ARE WE? WHAT ARE WE? WHAT *ARE* WE?!"

This torturous period can also be referred to as pre-relationship limbo. Other questions that tend to pop up during this limbo include:

- "Can we see other people?"

- "Where do you see this going?"

- "How would you feel about meeting my parents?"

- "I notice your relationship status still says 'single.'"

That last one is not so much a question, but if delivered in a passive-aggressive tone, it will sound like there should be a question mark at the end.

You would think that with time and the wisdom of age, this conversation gets easier to have. The truth is, the older you get, the trickier this is to navigate. When you were in grade school, a simple note asking the other person to check "Yes" or "No" if they liked you would suffice. High school dudes really had no game and tended to just straight-up ask: "So, you wanna be my girlfriend now?" after boob-groping their way through the latest *The Fast and the Furious* flick with you. What moments like these lacked in pizzazz or tact, they made up for in directness.

As you get older, you are expected to go on a million dates and then, only once you realize all of your stuff has slowly been transported to his place, do you feel confident enough to even introduce the thought of an "are we exclusive?" conversation into your brain. If your fear is that asking this question will scare a guy away, just remember, when a guy likes you, he is equally worried that you could move on and find someone else too. At a minimum, once you start sleeping with a guy, you are completely in the clear to ask where his dick has been (or is currently being). As Nike would advise you, *just do it.*

ALTERNATIVE LABELS

Still not sure he's your boyfriend? No worries! In the meantime, use these suggested titles when introducing your man.

"Hi everyone, I'd like you to meet my . . ."

- Main Melon
- Man of Honor
- Kind Sir
- Man-Friend
- Gentleman Caller
- Escort-Go
- Handsome One
- Special Friend . . . uh, not special as in like mentally challenged, just special to me, but not special in like a serious way . . . unless he wants to be serious, just, like, a casual special.
- Buddy Wuddy
- Sex Pal
- Guy Man Dude
- Bubba
- Booski
- Babesicle
- Boo Boo

MORAL OF THE STORY
ACTIONS SPEAK LOUDER THAN LABELS

Before you become preoccupied by your relationship status, recognize that everyone moves at different speeds and some guys take their "boyfriend" label more seriously than others. Some might want more time before committing to a label, but could simultaneously have no problem agreeing not to see other people. These arrangements are dumb and are like asking for "melted cheese bread" instead of a "grilled cheese." But, hey, at least you still got the sandwich. The important thing is how good that sandwich is; so, in other words, focus on the quality of your relationship before you focus on what you call it.

At the end of the day, labels only go so far. Labeling someone isn't always what locks them down. There are "boyfriends" who act like jerks and there are "I-don't-know-what-we-ares" who treat you like a queen. Just like how you can't trust that "All Natural" label on a box of fruit snacks that actually contain formaldehyde, the label of "boyfriend" is nothing more than fancy packaging. Only you know what's inside.

TIWYS

You're Too Worried About a Timeline

The Planner and the Vacation

You're the type of person who is on top of everything. Thank you notes are in the mail the day after you get a gift, phone bills are paid on time, and vacation days at work are requested months in advance. But currently you are having a major dilemma. Your vacation days are about to run out. And you *really* need to know if you're going to need them for something important. You explain this scenario to Andrés, the guy you've been dating long enough to have already met his parents, peed with the door open in front of, and talked with about names for your future dog together.

"I really love you," you tell Andrés, as you both sit in sweatpants on a Friday night while you watch an episode from your box set of *Freaks and Geeks* (RIP your youth).

"I love you too," he says.

"Great! Then you'll be able to help me with my problem," you say, as you tussle the man bun he's tied his dark brown locks in. "All of my friends want to do a girls' trip to Tulum this year for a week. That means I'll need to use all five of my last vacation days."

"Killer. A buddy of mine got back from a surfing trip in Tulum a couple months ago," he says. "I'll pull up his Instagram. You have to see this sunset pic he took, it's insane."

He doesn't get it. You snatch the phone out of his hand and try again.

"I'll need to use *all five* of my last vacation days," you repeat. "I won't have *any* left."

He stares at you blankly. You decide to spell it out for him. You speak loud, enunciating each word.

"I am figuring out if I should go on the trip or if I should save the vacation days for any *big* events that might come up. That's my problem."

Andrés looks around the room, confused. Your blood begins to boil.

"What's the problem?" he mumbles.

"I NEED TO KNOW IF YOU'RE GOING TO PROPOSE!"

"What?" he gulps. But before he can say anything else, you cut him off.

"I would obviously need to use the rollover vacation days for our wedding."

He gets up from his couch.

"Whoa—I said I wanted to get married one day. But I am not ready yet. What's the rush?"

"My grandpa's got two years tops left to live and I want him at my wedding," you say. "On top of that, I want to be married for at least one year before having kids, and they're building a new international preschool on the corner that's expected to be ready in the next twenty-five months. I want our kids to be children of the world. If we don't act fast, those spaces will fill up!"

"Are you listening to yourself right now?" he asks.

You aren't listening, you're too focused.

"Also, maybe we'd want to go to Tulum for our honeymoon. If we do, I wouldn't want to go with my friends. I would wait to go with you instead. For our honeymoon."

"There is no honeymoon! You are fifty steps ahead of me. I wasn't thinking about our children speaking Mongolian. I thought we'd look for a dog to adopt together and see how that went. But I wouldn't be surprised if you've already planned the dog we don't have's one-year birthday party."

"No, that would be crazy," you say. "But I did secure him or her a spot at Eco Doggie Day Care because it's hella competitive."

"Goodbye."

Andrés grabs his keys and exits his own apartment. You continue your rant.

"WAIT—I NEED TO KNOW IF YOU ARE PROPOSING SO I CAN FIGURE OUT MY TRAVEL PLANS. I AM A PLANNER, MOTHERFUCKER! DON'T YOU KNOW THAT ABOUT ME?"

You open the window and pop your head out to scream down the street at him.

"I JUST WANT TO LOOK HOT IN OUR WEDDING PHOTOS! YOU'VE SEEN MY MOM, I HAVE LIKE FOUR YEARS BEFORE I GET JOWLS."

Andrés drives away. You wait and wait for him to come back, but after a few years, gross maggots and creepy cobwebs move in and eventually the landlord decides to bulldoze his building.

You are still waiting by the window for Andrés to return as construction workers have you physically removed from the premises, despite your fervent attempt to latch on to the windowsill with both hands crying:

"I AM NOT . . . GOING . . . TO MAKE . . . MY TIMELINE." ●

Create *your own* TIMELINE

{ Connect the dots! Just like in a relationship, make up the order as you go and skip the milestones you don't want. }

You met him! START

You meet his weird friends and come up with an excuse for why you can't hook them up with your friends.

Delete all dating profiles.

You visit the ER together!

You meet his parents, who bestow strange gifts upon you, like charm bracelets and pocket mirrors.

Get drunk, throw up on his shoes, but he takes care of you—no judgies!

He's comfortable enough to tell you that you have a booger hanging from your nose.

Plan to adopt a dog together, but realize that you are both too selfish to care for a living thing.

You know who you'll grow old with.

You unsuccessfully try to merge your friend groups.

You take 362 hand selfies to get the perfect engagement ring photo. OMG, you're engaged!

He makes you one of his "favorites" in his iPhone.

Purchase tchotchkes together on international shores. First vaca!

He poops in your apartment.

He reflexively blurts out "I love you" when you find his missing wallet.

First inside joke!

You move in together. Panic attack when you realize you've sacrificed personal space for cheaper rent.

You start following wedding dress designers on Instagram . . . just in case.

You're his girl-friend! It's official. He never told you, but you overheard him tell his mom.

Four-hour crying match in IKEA over lighting fixtures.

LETTING GO OF CONTROL

Like any motivational poster (preferably one featuring a sleeping kitten wearing cozy jammies) will tell you, we're all like snowflakes—each person is unique. This means each timeline is different. Before you have a meltdown as you approach (fill in whatever age you've deemed unacceptable for singledom) years old, remember that it could be this exact anxiety that is creeping people out. You are worrying about things you have no control over. The way a dog can smell fear, people can smell desperation.

If one person meets the love of her life at nineteen and another meets that person at forty-five, does it mean one is happier than the other? If it does, then they are getting this life thing all wrong. It's the memories you make and adventures you have in between each milestone that count (cue the next motivational poster of a Golden Retriever puppy with sunglasses and a sombrero).

MORAL OF THE STORY

DON'T PLAN YOUR CHICKEN'S WEDDING BEFORE IT HATCHES

While we are sure you have a great idea for a choreographed first dance you know will go viral, hold up, sistah. Ask yourself this: Would I rather be engaged to someone who isn't ready and is unsure about this relationship just for the sake of hitting my timeline, or would I rather wait for the right person and enter into this happy union with confidence on both sides? Mull it over.

You may be tempted to start dropping hints. That's cool. A conversation about what you want for the future is important. But waving your hand in his face and telling him that if he likes it then he better put a ring on it is probably not the most tactful approach. No offense, Beyoncé. Queen B. Almighty Beyoncé. Your Majesty, our apologies.

Baby-making is a popular final stop on the romantic timeline. Ladies can be divided on this milestone. For some (who have likely witnessed a screaming child at Red Lobster), kids are not a part of the perfect package. For others, they will only date a guy if his last name sounds good with the names they've already chosen for their future children together. For those in the later category, remember: We are living in the future. There are so many choices for having children late in life. Freeze your eggs! Adopt! Whatever.

We are talking about creating a new living being with someone. Is this really something you want to rush into with a guy who might not be in the picture in a few years? Know what's more expensive than IVF when you're forty-three? A custody battle with some d-bag you let inseminate you too early on. The only time it's okay to rush your conception? If you're trying to plan so that you start to show around Halloween and can incorporate the baby bump into your costume. That is an acceptable plan we support and think is brilliant.

TIWYS

You Don't Have a Good Wingman

The Hero and the Villain

The place is packed, boisterous, and lively. There's a New Orleans brass band playing in the center surrounded by patrons chugging down jugs of various German brews and stuffing their faces with bratwursts and giant pretzels. You try not to spill beer out of your boot glass as you shimmy through the crowd and find your way back to the table inside the beer garden (excuse you, *biergarten*).

"Thanks so much for inviting me," you say to Andy, your brown-eyed and grinning new co-worker who invited you here. "This place has been on our list to check out forever."

"Yeah, I love this place," he replies. "I'm sorry. Did you say *our*?"

"Oh yeah. My roommate Carol just got here. I hope that's okay."

Carol pushes her way through the crowd with her broad shoulders. In her wake, angry hipsters regain their footing after being smacked by both her body and her oversized computer bag.

"This place smells and the music sucks," she whines, as she wipes pieces of her bedraggled dark hair off her sweaty face. "We're gonna go soon, right?"

You brought her along as a wingman, unsure if this was actually a date.

Andy, who had intended for this to be a date from the start, immediately recognizes your roommate for what she really is: a cockblock.

"I have a bunch of laundry to do in the morning so we can't stay out too late," Carol tells you. "Like another half hour, then we're good, yeah?"

Andy knows all too well how this scenario tends to go: As long as Carol is here, he doesn't stand chance with you. Just as he suspects, you immediately turn away from him and immerse yourself in deep conversation with Carol, hoping she will lighten up and want to stay.

He is about to give up. Cockblocks are evil supervillains. Andy sulks and prepares to say his goodbyes when his best buddy, Wyatt, bursts through the crowd. SWOOSH!

"Wingman to the rescue!" he announces, as he whips his red parka off with a flourish. "I possess the social skills, relentlessness, and high blood alcohol level necessary to battle the treacherous forces of evil, who are blocking my friend Andy from getting laid."

"Man, you could not have come at a better time," says Andy, pointing to the true archnemesis of Wyatt the Wingman: Carol the Cockblock. "I could really use your help right about now. I am literally dying out there with this chick."

Wyatt runs a hand through his perfectly coiffed black hair and gives Andy a knowing wink before flying into action.

"Anybody want shots?" he asks the crowd. "I'm buying!" KAPOW!

You flip your head around, ditching Carol in the middle of her story about her call with Comcast.

Carol mutters, "It's weird how that guy Andy kind of looks like your dad, huh?"

You do a double take as you gulp the shot of tequila. It's kind of true. Hmm . . .

"She is a monster," Andy whispers to Wyatt.

Wyatt is unfazed. He knows just how to keep the conversation fun while flattering both the target (you) and the obstacle (Carol the Cockblock).

"You ladies are prettier than half the actresses in Hollywood," praises Wyatt. "In fact, you look like the girl on this show I was just watching." BAM!

Andy jumps in. "Totally like the girl on the show." KABOO—

"Is the show called *Young, Beautiful and Vanished*?" Carol interrupts.

"I, uh, don't think I know that show," says Wyatt.

"It's a true crime series about young, beautiful girls that go to bars and go home with strange guys," explains Carol. "Want to guess how most episodes end? Spoiler alert: they vanish."

She isn't Wyatt the Wingman's archnemesis for nothing. Andy panics and pulls Wyatt aside.

"Wyatt, that cockblock is indestructible. Carol is the Mussolini of misery. Should we abort the mission?"

Wyatt pulls something out of the utility belt wrapped around his waist. "Not to fear, citizen. I've come prepared."

He slides a pair of goggles onto his face. The bottle-thick lenses blur his vision. Beer goggles! He's ready to make the ultimate sacrifice for his brother in arms.

"Can I have this dance?" Wyatt asks Carol.

ZAP! Wyatt the Wingman woos Carol the Cockblock. He dances with her, makes out with her, compliments her on obscure things that normally only another woman would notice, like her eyebrows. POW! POW! POW! And this is how Carol the Cockblock's reign of terror comes to an end. You and your guy are finally safe to grope and fondle wherever you so choose. Wyatt the Wingman may not be the hero we deserve, but he is definitely the hero we need. ●

Letter to a Wingman

BEING A WINGMAN IS A TIME-
HONORED TRADITION; THE
ULTIMATE GOOD SPORT. BUT
WITH GREAT POWER COMES
GREAT RESPONSIBILITY.
AFTER DESIGNATING YOUR
WINGMAN, PULL HER ASIDE
FOR A PRIVATE MOMENT AND
PASS ALONG THIS ANCIENT
ARTIFACT: A LETTER FROM
THE WING SOCIETY.

Dear Wingman,

This letter is to congratulate you on your acceptance into an elite society—a society composed of trusted purse-holders and snappy small-talk-makers. Though there were many candidates, you have been chosen based on your unique ability to say "yes" when invited along to meet your friend's potential new romantic interest. You may not have asked to join this society and instead, were lured under a false pretense ("We're overdue for a girls' night!", "Post-work sangria?"). Whatever brought you here, welcome.

We are here to tell it to you straight. As a Wingman, you are merely a prop to ease your friend's social anxiety, provide her with symmetry on the dance floor, and aid in case an emergency shall arise (she gets stood up).

Things to bring along for the night:

1. Drink money (as the Wingman, it's likely your friend's date will only pay for her)
2. Gum (not for yourself)
3. Hairspray (also not for yourself)

4. A list of quirky and endearing stories about your friend that are designed to make her sound charming and down-to-earth

5. An eBook (or just an actual book. No one will be paying any attention to you at all so it really doesn't matter what you're doing. Go for broke, and bring the complete works of James Patterson)

6. Cab money (hunny, you're going home alone)

7. Comfortable shoes (in case you never find that cab)

8. Pajamas and earplugs if your friend's guy ends up doing one of those "hey-ladies-let's-all-go-back-to-my-house-for-a-drink-but-this-really-means-I-want-to-fuck-one-of-you-and-I-don't-know-how-to-tell-the-other-one-to-leave"

While you may feel like merely an insignificant supporting character in someone else's larger fairy-tale romance (think Kevin Connolly in *The Notebook*. Remember when he died? That was so sad!), always remember you are an integral part of the dating scene. Things would not work without you. You are doing a noble, selfless thing, like feeding the homeless or spending a day building schools for poor children in Uganda. Helping your friend get laid will make you a better, stronger, and kinder person. Also, now that bitch owes you! You could potentially milk this thing for free dinner or unlimited access to her fancy building's free washer/dryer. This is a cause worth your time and dedication. Wing on, Winglady!

Sincerely,

President of The Trusted Sisterhood of the Wing Society (U.S. chapter)

WHAT IF YOU'RE BEING COCKBLOCKED?

The most important thing after finding a good wingman is to be aware of cockblocks. Here's how to deal with someone who's keeping you away from a guy you want.

TYPES OF COCKBLOCKS

The Female: Blocking tends to rely on complaints and passive-aggressive putdowns. Examples may include: "My feet hurt." or "Aren't you on your period?" or "He's a good fit for you. You like guys with fucked-up noses, right?" The motivation for this type of cockblock is usually due to already being in a relationship, seeing no potential prospects for herself, or extreme hunger.

Occasionally, the female cockblock is secretly interested in your target, often called The "I Want That Cock" Cockblock or The Competition Cockblock. This is the most difficult cockblock to stop.

The Male: He is simply ever-present. Unlike the female, the male is overly friendly—so friendly that he won't leave his friend's side and allow you the opportunity to make a move. Alcohol may be impairing this individual's awareness of social cues, although in many cases the guy is actually just an insufferable dickhead. Frequently, the male cockblock is also referred to as The Oblivious Cockblock. He's drunk, he thinks it's just "a bro's night," and he has no idea he is destroying some serious game.

HOW TO SPOT A COCKBLOCK

The cockblock is a chameleon and therefore may be tricky to spot initially: male or female, skinny or fat, well-adjusted or batshit crazy. It is important to note factors such as body position (specifically, positioned between the interested parties). Excuses to get your love interest away from you can vary: a smoke break, a bathroom buddy, a personal crisis that needs immediate one-on-one advice, or wanting to show off new swing dance moves on the dance floor. Whatever the reason, he or she will strategically pull your target away from you and out of sight.

Bringing a wingman along with you is your strongest ammunition against a cockblock. We find that having a game plan and clearly explaining your goals to a potential cockblock may help the evening run a bit more smoothly (this works best if you are dealing with The Oblivious Cockblock but can backfire if you are dealing with The Competition Cockblock). If that doesn't seem to be working, attempt to make an Irish exit along with your romantic interest. When in doubt, hire a hitman.

ARE YOU A COCKBLOCK?

Fun fact: One out of three people can be categorized as a cockblock. Look to your left, look to your right. If neither of those people are blocking cock (and, coincidentally, those two people are on a date that you interrupted), you are probably the cockblock. It happens. If this is the case, we highly recommend you check yourself before you wreck yourself. A good friend wants to see her friend happy. You are young and cute for a cruelly short period of time in life, so just enjoy your night and have fun.

Exceptions to the Rule

It is a piss-poor type of lady who would leave you stranded at a dive bar with no means of getting home just so she can get some. If you realize you are friends with a gal who won't go anywhere without the motivation of "manhunting" and will dump you at all costs, the scenario has changed. You are no longer deemed a cockblock if you are blocking in the name of what is sane and fair. That shitty friend doesn't need a wingman, she needs a hobby (other than men). A friend who spoils your one-on-one time every single night you hang out needs a little cockblocking in her life to keep her straight. Find a new friend for whom you would happily wing or who would happily wing for you. Flap your wings and fly free, little birdie.

MORAL OF THE STORY

NO BIRD SOARS TOO HIGH IF HE SOARS WITH HIS OWN WINGMAN

Your approach to wingmen should be like your approach to condoms: Don't assume a guy has one, so bring your own. A wingman—which is not a gender-specific term—will unselfishly fan the flames of a budding romantic fire for her friend. She is confident enough to hold her own once you've paired off and will keep a positive attitude, rooting for you to get it in.

It's Not Relationship Season

The News and the Weather

The hot summer sun glares at you through the kitchen window in your apartment, taunting you. You should be enjoying the first perfect day of the season, but you're bored. All of your friends have mysteriously gone out of town last minute and it's eerily quiet outside. You listlessly flip through the channels on your TV until you come upon a breaking news report from Sam Stone at Channel 7 News.

News 7 Los Angeles

Sam Stone: We interrupt this regularly scheduled program with a developing story. We are getting more information on the massive migration of women from warmer states to regions that remain cold all year round. This week a *U.S. News & World Report* study came out on a phenomenon known as Cuffing Season. The study states that "98.7% of males tested in warm-weather climates preferred to be single. But when those same males were placed in cold-weather

climates, they immediately searched for a partner to cozy up with and engage in activities
such as rewatching *Mad Men*, having the kind of
sex where you leave your socks on, and other
hallmarks of a monogamous relationship." In
response, women are seeking out colder climates in order to find men who want to settle
down. We have never seen such a sudden reaction
to the release of any study in the history of
studies. For more on this shocking trend, we
go to Erica Abrego, who is live on the scene in
Anchorage, Alaska.

Erica Abrego: I'm here with one of the migrators
who recently left her home in Dallas, Texas.
Colleen, what made you decide to migrate?

Colleen: Do you know how many guys I've dated
who have broken up with me before the summer?
I was dating this one guy last year. We started
going out around September, and by October he
was officially introducing me as his girlfriend. Things were going great. Then out of
nowhere he started acting distant in March. Two
months later, he's posting pictures of himself
riding jet skis with tan girls in bikinis and
I'm single and learning how to ice-fish.

Sam Stone: Unbelievable story, Erica. Now I'd
like to share a brief interview with small
business owner Joe O'Conner, thanks to our sister station in Atlanta, Georgia. Joe is closing

his frozen yogurt shop after twenty-three years on Peachtree Street.

Joe O'Conner: Men don't eat froyo. It's the girls! Where'd they all go? I ain't never seen anything like it!

Sam Stone: Absolutely devastating. Here with the latest on this week's weather is our meteorologist Bri Windly. Bri, what's your spin?

Bri Windly: As you can see here, the migration patterns of single women coincide with the cold front the Northeast experienced over the past few days. With Toronto preparing for a blizzard, you can expect to see a dramatic spike of single women looking for visas and Canadian blizzard boyfriends. This sudden migration has triggered a devastating crisis to many subtropical economies.

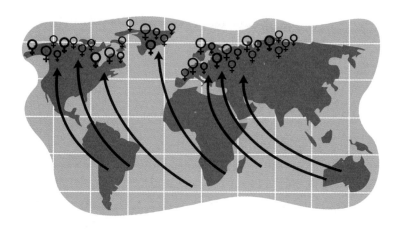

Sam Stone: Now we take you back to Erica Abrego in Anchorage, Alaska.

Erica Abrego: Thank you, Sam. I'm here with another migrator. Janine, tell us about your travels.

Janine: The media and those bloggers have it all wrong! It's not just the men. Women get antsy in the warmer months too! I was always finding an excuse to break up with guys before the summer so I could go on a girls' trip to my friend's beach house in Malibu. I didn't want to be *that* girl who always had to bring her boyfriend around for fun summer trips, you know? I wanted to be single.

Erica Abrego: So why did you migrate?

Janine: I knew I was going to fall back into that same pattern if I stayed in Malibu for the summer again. I needed to trick my body into wanting to be in a relationship. So I left and chose a place that will never get hot again. I'm constantly freezing, which means I constantly want to cuddle.

Erica Abrego: Sam, back to you in the studio.

Sam Stone: I just have to say, Erica—that was an incredibly moving interview. What a brave, brave woman. Instead of giving up and waiting an entire year for the next round of icy cold, she is chasing the cold. These women are true storm chasers.

You flip the channel off and log into Facebook. Sure enough, all of your single friends are posting photos from their new locations throughout the Arctic. They're dressed like snow bunnies, with fur-trimmed jackets, beanies, and snow boots. You immediately begin packing your bags and post your apartment on Airbnb. Goodbye, Cali. Hello space heaters, dog sleds, and hand-holding with a mountain man. ●

DATING BY THE CALENDAR

Every year when winter hits, the animal kingdom reacts like clockwork. Bears go into hibernation, birds fly south, and single humans . . . search for someone special to watch Netflix with. Similarly, once the weather starts to get warmer, cicadas buzz, mosquitoes bite, and coupled humans . . . dump their special someone and wear as little clothing as possible.

If you find that both you and many of those around you are single with no prospects on the horizon, it is very possible that you have simply missed the cutoff date for something known as Cuffing Season. Everyone has been paired off and there are no single men left to go around. It's not your fault. The calendar is working against you.

On top of already wanting a significant other to cuddle with on cold winter nights, the holidays only amplify this desire. It begins with Halloween in October when you start searching Buzzfeed for couples costume ideas (Vanna White and a *Wheel of Fortune* board—genius!). Then it's Thanksgiving (you'll be giving thanks that you're not flying solo when you run into old high school hookups at the local bar back home). Then it's Hanukkah and Christmas (you already bought him a gift and you don't want store credit to Bass Pro). You can't make out with yourself on New Year's, and Valentine's Day is, well, the holiday of love. There truly is no better time to be with someone than from October to February. After that, the holidays are over and it's a warm-weather breakup free-for-all.

Holidays Worth Staying Together For

Is that string of winter holidays from Halloween to Valentine's Day the only thing holding you and your man together? Take a look at these underappreciated romantic holidays for couples who need an excuse to keep the lovey-dovey celebrations going all year round.

Date	Holiday	Reason
March 5	Multiple Personality Day	It's just like role-playing in bed but better!
March 16	Everything You Do Is Right Day	What's the point of being right if you have no one to fight with?
May 8	Lost Sock Memorial Day	Together, our two solo socks will make a pair.
May 12	Limerick Day	*There once was a girl and her man / Their relationship was going to plan / But then he was dumb / Called quit on their run / And lived alone in a creepy van*
3rd Sunday in June	Father's Day	I clearly have daddy issues and you are filling the void.
June 26	Take Your Dog to Work Day	Break up with me and I'm taking the fucking dog.
July 27	Take Your Plants for a Walk Day	Won't you be sad when your begonias are the only ones at the park without a mommy?
August 5	National Oyster Day	Oysters are an aphrodisiac. You're going to eat them and be so horny and you'll be glad you have a girlfriend.
August 13	Left Hander's Day	That hand had to do a lot more work when you were single.
October 1	International Day for the Elderly	Let's grow old together!

MORAL OF THE STORY

IT'S NOT YOU, IT'S THE WEATHER

Don't be discouraged by a seemingly random pre-summer dumping. That douchey dude is thinking with his thermometer (phallic symbol!) and not his heart. Take a breather, enjoy the sunshine, and wait for the right guy. Once you have a real connection with someone, nothing can stop it, not even Mother Nature. Learn how to spot the difference between a seasonal fling and the real deal. Danny Zuko was willing to leave the T-Birds and start running high school track for his summer-lovin' squeeze. That's about as real as it gets.

TIWYS

You Don't Know How to Compromise

The Bro and the Bride

A couple of weeks ago, your college sweetheart Jake got down on one knee and asked you to marry him. Now it's time to plan your dream wedding. You arrive with Jake at the offices of acclaimed wedding planner, Teddy La Rocca.

"I've been planning weddings for years and whatever your dreams are, whatever fantastical wedding you dream up—I will make it happen," Teddy boasts in a silvery tone.

You gaze around in wonder. It's a girly paradise. You grasp the arm of your former-hockey-playing fiancé. He's a good guy to give up his Sunday afternoon to come talk vegetarian options and seating arrangements.

"Babe, I have a surprise," Jake says as he reaches into his backpack and hands you a heavy book.

"I made this scrapbook to help plan our nuptials. We're going to have the dankest wedding!"

You scan the album. He has pasted clippings from the pages of his favorite magazines: *Sports Illustrated*, *Esquire*, and *PC Gamer* to create his own wedding-themed fifty-page scrapbook.

"Oh, that's really sweet you're showing effort," you say, confused but also thoroughly impressed by the handiwork. "I can't believe you made this whole thing in just two weeks."

"Babe, I started this when I was twelve. I've been dreaming about my wedding since I was a tiny bro. I'm so pumped!"

You were under the assumption men didn't care about weddings unless they were a rare groomzilla like Kanye West. Teddy, intrigued by this rare case of groom enthusiasm, unbuttons his light pink seersucker suit jacket, picks up the book, and begins to flip through it.

"Guests enter reception through an arc shaped like the doors of the starship Enterprise."

"Two words: warp speed," Jake says.

"Whoa, whoa, whoa," you stammer. "Honey, I appreciate your, uh, creativity but I'm not sure that will work with the ten dozen pink tulips."

The wedding planner continues to read.

"Waiters dressed as superheroes from *The Avengers*. Exotic!"

Great, apparently your wedding is becoming a themed frat party. Teddy seems to think Jake's ideas are fantastic. He's also likely tallying up the costs for such an extraordinary affair.

"A beer pong tournament with Natty Ice," he continues. "Maybe we can try Moët. Champagne pong!"

You want to compromise, but you haven't been curating a Pinterest wedding board for naught.

"Beer pong?" you deadpan. "I bought a $6,000 Vera Wang gown!"

"Look, people get drunk at weddings!" Jake contests. "That's what you do, babe. You're the one who said your friends only dance when they're drunk. I'm thinking outside the box here."

"A hockey rink!" Teddy gushes, flipping further along in the book. "Bring on the Zambonis!"

"What? No! No Zambonis," you plead.

"Picture it: right in the center of the reception," Jake explains, grabbing a pen and a sheet of custom Teddy La Rocca stationery off the desk to scribble a floor plan.

"And a poker tournament!" Teddy reads. "We'll make it Monaco-themed! *Chic-chic!*"

"Gambling at our wedding?" you ask, utterly baffled.

"I was also thinking, the *Indiana Jones* theme song for the first dance would be off the hook!"

"No."

"Tables shaped like pirate ships?"

"No."

"Can I bring my Xbox?"

"No."

"Comic book programs?"

"No."

"An ice sculpture—"

"Sure."

"—of Chewbacca!"

"No!"

Jake begins pacing back and forth. He's fuming. He wants to know why you refuse to compromise.

"I expected to compromise on the main course and what color napkins to have!" you scream.

"I don't even like using napkins!" he yells back.

Teddy is frazzled, likely worried this wedding planning gig might be over before it starts. He tries to calm you both down.

"No! I will not calm down!" Jake cries. "This is some legit bro sadness. I put a lot of thought into this, babe. You love Michael Bublé, mimosas, and tilapia—done! I love beer bongs, video games, and Chewbacca—done! See? Compromise! I just, I love you so much. I want this day to be a testament of our love. I want our wedding to be . . . baller."

He is shaken and upset. You realize what a hypocrite you've been.

"When you put it that way, I guess it's not that crazy," you tell him. "I didn't realize you've been dreaming this up since you were a, a, a—"

"A tiny bro."

"Right. A tiny bro. Look, I'm sorry, baby. I want to compromise. I want our wedding to be about both of us."

Eight months later, you walk down the aisle to Michael Bublé's "Everything," sung by a Metallica cover band. The bridesmaids wear mint tulle gowns and the groomsmen are dressed as Storm Troopers. You have a five-tier wedding cake by Milk Bar and your programs look like a *Sin City* comic book. You have ten dozen pink tulips on each table and a *Call of Duty* tournament in the corner. It's not exactly what you imagined, but it's a representation of both of you. ●

YOU'RE SUPPOSED TO BE DIFFERENT

The Spice Girls spent a lot of time singing about when "2 Become 1." While they are widely known for their sound dating advice ("I wanna really really really wanna zigazig ha" is a phrase that has saved many marriages), two becoming one is actually not very advisable in a healthy relationship. Differences keep things interesting and compromising keeps you both happy.

If you're feeling down about disagreements, just remember: Those contrasting ideas, thoughts, and opinions combined are what makes a relationship a relationship and different from living life alone—where you drink directly out of an orange juice container, and no one ever leaves the toilet seat up or makes you turn off *Dancing with the Stars* because they want to go to sleep (oh wait, that all sounds pretty awesome. That wasn't the point.). The point is, you shouldn't want to date yourself because that gets boring. You do you. Let him do him. But always remember to do each other.

How to Compromise

You	He	Compromise
Start a book club.	Starts a fight club.	After an intriguing dissection of the latest John Grisham novel, your friends exchange blows to decide who picks next week's book.
Enjoy walking around the farmers' market on the weekend.	Plays flag football with the boys on Sundays.	Give him a concussion when he least expects it as you hike a baby squash toward him at the market. Just like football! Samesies.
Throw a low-key New Year's Eve dinner party.	Goes to a rager at the Cosmopolitan in Las Vegas.	Throw a dinner party at home but hire a tough bouncer to guard the door and charge all of his friends a cover fee but let your girlfriends in for free.
Are a planner who is married to your iCal.	Is a free spirit who craves spontaneity.	Pencil in some time between 2:17–4:01 P.M. on Saturday to do something completely unexpected.
Are a big fan of Facebook.	Doesn't "get" social media.	Delete your account, but text your boyfriend frequent "status updates" regarding your candid opinion on politics, movie trailers, and personal pet peeves. He doesn't have to respond, but should at least express if he likes it.
Celebrate Christmas.	Celebrates Hanukkah.	Raise your kids to be godless heathens (kidding! just buy them lots of presents).

MORAL OF THE STORY **IT IS BETTER TO BEND THAN TO BREAK UP**

If you love someone, you should understand that his opinion on something is valid (even if it's valid and *wrong*). There are not many disagreements that are incapable of being resolved by finding a middle ground. If you don't resolve these disagreements in the moment, they will resurface when you least expect them. This means compromising on the small stuff, like chicken teriyaki versus chicken cacciatore and whether to re-watch season two or three of *Breaking Bad* . . . and on the bigger stuff, like family, money, religion, and sex. Fulfilling the other person's needs does not mean sacrificing your own individuality. If he cares about you, he will be just as motivated to accommodate your wants and needs as well.

You Want a Rom-Com Romance

The Script and the Star

FADE IN:

EXT. ITALIAN RESTAURANT - NIGHT

We open on a young man and woman dining at an outdoor table in a hip, bustling neighborhood. ISAAC (mid-20s, laid-back, smart, handsome) and MATILDA (mid-20s, girl next door, loveable) lean in to each other. Each displays the kind of overeager attentiveness indicative of a first date.

> ISAAC
> So anyway, that's when I decided to do something I never dreamed of. I packed up and moved out here to San Francisco!

MATILDA

I think that's really brave. You know what they say: Those who cannot change their minds—

BOTH

Cannot change anything!

ISAAC

That's so strange. My mom used to say that all the time. It was my high school yearbook quote.

MATILDA

You've got to be joking me. That was my high school yearbook quote!

ISAAC and MATILDA lock eyes and stare at each other in disbelief. They hold the stare until MATILDA blushes and looks down. ISAAC gently takes her hand and grins.

MUSIC SWELLS.

ISAAC

I guess it's meant to be then. Hey, I know this might sound crazy since we just met and all, but I think I'm really falling for you.

MATILDA

It does sound crazy, but I think I might be falling for you too.

A gust of wind blows MATILDA'S bangs over her
eyes and ISAAC brushes the hair out of her
face and caresses it.

> ISAAC
> I want to learn everything there
> is to know about you.

> MATILDA
> Ask me anything. I'm an open book.

> ISAAC
> Okay. Um. What do you, like, do
> for fun?

"Cut!" you scream.

Here we go again. Another rogue date, going off script and improvising. If he were following along with *The Script*, he would see that his next line clearly reads, "What was the most defining moment of your childhood?" You've brought along *The Script*, a 127-page leather-bound document, to every date you've ever been on. No one has been able to stay on book but you know when the right guy comes along, he will know what the lines are supposed to be.

You decide to cut Isaac some slack at this audition and give him a prompt.

"Psst," you whisper. "I think what you meant to ask me was something about my childhood?"

"Huh? You want to talk about your childhood?"

You try a different tactic.

"What's your character's motivation?" you ask.

"My motivation? I don't know what you mean. I'm just looking to meet a nice girl."

"Oooh, I like that last line. I'm gonna make a note to add that into my next draft."

"What?"

You roll your eyes. You decide to skip ahead a few scenes to move things along.

"Let's go back to my place," you tell him.

Isaac picks up the bill (maybe he *does* know the script after all!) and you head back to your apartment together. As you unlock the door and turn around to say, "Thank you for a lovely evening," as specified on page 63, he follows you in.

"What are you doing?" you bark at him.

"I, uh, assumed you wanted me to come in," he stammers. "Sorry, I don't mean to be too forward. You just seemed really eager and I—"

"Scene 52B!" you yell, before slamming the door in his face.

Isaac stands bewildered in the cold. He turns to leave, then doubles back around and raises a hand to ring the doorbell. He rethinks this move and sits down on the stoop, scratching his head.

INT. MATILDA'S LIVING ROOM - NIGHT

OLIVIA (mid-20s, Matilda's roommate, sassy and cool) sits next to MATILDA on their living room couch.

> OLIVIA
> Just go for it, already. Stop him
> at the airport before he gets on
> that plane!

You explain to Olivia that he's outside of the apartment and that the whole airport climax doesn't happen until later, but you're glad to see she's nailing her part.

"What are you waiting for?" you shout from the window down to the street at Isaac.

"Do you want me to leave?" Isaac yells up to you.

"No! I want you to ring my doorbell and hold up a sign that says, 'To me, you are perfect,' while you play a recording of children Christmas caroling!"

"I am really confused. Why would I do that?"

"I'm sorry, I don't mean to overdirect you. Everyone has their own creative process. Do you want to just take this from the top?"

"Yes," he sighs. "That would be great. We were having a really nice night together and then things just got kinda weird. Let's just start the night over."

"No, no, no! Let's take this from the *very* top. Like the day we met. Honestly, I'd like you to try a different delivery of the line, 'Is there anything I can help you with?' after I enter the bookshop."

Isaac stares at you for a full minute. You don't flinch. He then turns to leave.

"Wait! Where are you going?" you shout. "You're not supposed to leave me until we have our fight in the canoe after I find out my mother was hiding your letters to me and then we kiss in the rain. Then you read my diary and leave me again and I have to chase you in my tiger-print undies in the snow to try to win you back. Then we have a fight about sex complicating our relationship and you leave again, but on New Year's Eve you run to meet me just before the clock strikes twelve and tell me that I'm the last person you want to talk to before you go to sleep at night. And everything is great again. Isaac? Isaac!" ●

THE MOVIES LIE

In a rom-com, streets are mysteriously wet on a perfectly sunny day, the leading man never wakes up with horrendous morning breath, and your romantic competition never turns out to actually be a pretty sweet girl with no master plan to embarrass you at a party. The silver screen is not the standard to which you should hold your own romantic expectations. You're not a bird, he didn't have you at hello, and sometimes you just have to put Baby in a corner for her own good.

On a smaller scale (and screen), you may be tempted to compare your relationship to the perfect ones you see on social media, and try to model yours after those seemingly rom-com-ready romances. Here's the thing: No one Instagrams photos of their awkward first dates or their divorce court hearings. A picture may be worth a thousand words, but in the case of Instagram, all those words are dirty lies—they're lying by omission.

MORAL OF THE STORY

YOU CAN'T ALWAYS GET WHAT YOU WATCH

If you enter into a relationship with a playbook of exactly what moves a guy should make, you will always be let down. Relationships are like an improv scene: You can attempt to guide the scene, but how a person responds is out of your control. If you've ever sat through a bad improv set, you know that watching an actor force his agenda leads to an excruciatingly painful experience for everyone involved. If you enter a scene with the entire scenario mapped out ahead of time, you will be sorely disappointed when your scene partner initiates with, "I think my dog has Lepto. I hope you can help him, doctor!" and you still respond with, "I'm just a doctor of love! I don't even like animals." Congratulations, you just murdered a dog.

Your most successful relationship could very well look absolutely nothing like what you had initially dreamed of as your "perfect" romance. It won't be a romantic comedy because it's IRL, but most of the time real life is even better than anything an underpaid script doctor could dream up at a Starbucks.

ROMANTIC COMEDIES GET REAL

Pretty Woman
A prostitute (Julia Roberts) hooks up with a prominent rich businessman (Richard Gere), takes a selfie of him snorting cocaine off her vagina, and then sends it to TMZ in return for $100,000.

The Notebook
A young country boy (Ryan Gosling) and a rich Southern heiress (Rachel McAdams) have a summer fling. It was fun and all, but they grow up, she realizes they had absolutely nothing in common as teenagers, and doesn't think about him again. Years later, she finds out he built a house for her, is completely creeped out, and gets a restraining order.

How to Lose a Guy in 10 Days
An advertising executive (Matthew McConaughey) is told by co-workers he can oversee an advertising campaign if he wins a bet: Make a girl (Kate Hudson) fall in love with him in ten days. He laughs (obviously his co-workers are joking) and then sulks, and has to wait another two years before he gets that promotion. Meanwhile, that girl, an aspiring political writer at a *Cosmopolitan*-esque magazine, quits her job the day her editor assigns her to write a piece on "How to Lose a Guy in 10 Days."

Knocked Up
Career-ambitious Alison Scott (Katherine Heigl) gets pregnant after a one-night stand with a deadbeat stoner (Seth Rogen). She gets an abortion.

Never Been Kissed
A copyeditor (Drew Barrymore) gets an assignment to go undercover as a new student at a high school, where she thinks English teacher (Michael Vartan) is hot stuff. For various legal and logical reasons, this adult woman is unable to pretend to be a sixteen-year-old student, which becomes apparent after a student calls her out for being "an old bitch." The most hip thing she learns during her brief time hanging with teenagers is that print media is dead and she should probably look for a new job.

Acknowledgments

Thank you:

To Benjamin Blake for being a big brother, friend, manager, and fairy godfather all in one. You asked us what we wanted to do and made it happen. Chelsea Lindman for believing in the book. Jacquie Katz and the CAA team for seeing our potential. Brendan O'Neill and the Adams Media team for buying the book and giving us the freedom to be a little weird. Laura Daly for your patience and editor X-ray vision.

To the Peoples Improv Theater, you are truly our home. Chris Aurilio for providing a learning environment that allowed us to find our passion and find each other, Kevin Laibson for supporting us as artists, Keith Huang for giving us that first show date, and the Sketch 101 crew—that was really fun.

To our *This Is Why You're Single* boys: Morgan Ferretti, Matthew Robert Gehring, and Andrew Kimler, you are immensely talented and dashing, which is why we always wrote makeout scenes with you. Thanks for being our boyfriend, ex-boyfriend, dad, child, grandfather, grandchild, boss, bartender, private investigator, cab, bald eagle, dancing robot, angel, pilgrim, dreidel, Santa, sea captain, fiancé, suitor, bank robber, waiter, choreographer, and prince. You brought it all to life.

To the following people who helped support *This Is Why You're Single* along the way: Charley Brucato, James Carr, Archana Kumar, Steve Soroka, Scott Swayze, Brooks Wheelan, Michelle Wolf, Keisha Zollar, and the cast of our holiday video.

To Armando Zubieta, who is used to shooting beautiful supermodels but happily shot all of our mascara-smeared, champagne-guzzling, chip-eating, hot mess photos for every show and this book. We are in awe of your kindness.

To Lucie Rice for taking our illustrative ideas, making them awesome, and being gracious when faced with requests like "let's add more drool."

To Brad and Corey Howell for crossing state lines to collaborate on various projects and being cheerleaders on this one.

To the Upright Citizens Brigade for helping hone our comedic sensibilities.

To the staff at Argo Tea (a.k.a. our writers' room), we apologize for never letting you clock out on time.

To the friends who will always be members of our too-large pack and offered thoughtful feedback, support, or occasional inspiration: Jen Birn, Amanda Champagne-Meadows, Sandy Chansamone, Oliver Coleman, Lance Debler, Michelle Edgar, Whitney English, Jonathan Epstein, Molly Lane Epstein, Ashley Falzone, Cristina Gibson, Katie Haller, Nicole Hanriot, Charles Holloway, Lindsay Hubbard, Kiran Josen, Ashley Levy, Steven Loehr, Christina Mannino, Mark Marino, Olivia Melikhov, John Mothershead, Darla Murray, Eloise Parker, Kaitlyn Piccoli, Mary Beth Quirk, the Radkowskys, the Rodriguezes, Renee Saccente,

Ali Schwartz, Jennifer Shulman, Melissa Singer, Matt Sullivan, Katie Thiele, Erin Wagoner, Jen Weiner, Jennifer Weiss, Tara Weiss, and Jenna Yarema.

To our moms and dads (Lindy & Bill, Rita & Robert) and family, we love you. Please ignore the chapter about sex.

Samo the dog for being our muse.

Ian, you're a knucklehead.

Nic, you're my favorite person.

About the

LAURA LANE

is a comedy writer and performer. She is a correspondent at *People* and has written for ESPN, *Esquire*, and *Vanity Fair*, and held editor positions at *OK!*, *In Touch*, and *Life & Style*. She hosted the poker show *ESPN Inside Deal* and appeared in episodes of Morgan Spurlock's web series, *Mansome*, as well as shows on MTV, VH1, CNN, MSNBC, and Fox News. She studied sketch and improv at the Upright Citizens Brigade and Peoples Improv Theater and graduated from the University of Southern California where she won *Rolling Stone* magazine's college journalism contest for entertainment reporting. After writing a show and book about being single, Laura got engaged on stage while wearing a shirt that read: "#SINGLE". Her husband is incredibly hot. lauralane.com @LauraLane__

THISISWHYYOURESINGLESHOW.COM